SARAH LEAMY

VAN LIFE

Exploring the Northwest

with two dogs and a cat

in a van

SARAH LEAMY

ISBN-13: 978-1540359445

ISBN-10: 1540359441

OTHER BOOKS BY

SARAH LEAMY

WHEN NO ONE'S LOOKING

LUCKY SHOT

LUCKY FIND

LIVING THE DREAM

BRING A CHAINSAW

ACKNOWLEDGMENTS

I'd like to thank all who have encouraged my travels
and writing both. There are some incredibly special
communities, forums, and friends who have all helped
keep me going, finding me places to stay, roads to take,
giving pep talks on the bad days,
and sharing beers on the good days.

I thank each of you.

PROLOGUE

"I hate you! I hate you! What are you doing to me? Let me out. Let Me Out!"

Stevie flung himself from window to window, screaming, yowling, and scratching. Full on panic attack. Harold hid out of the way on the bed in the back, as much as a 65 # Akita/ Collie mix can hide within a small camper van. He whimpered. His tummy growled. Rosie sat in the passenger seat, her head swinging from side to side as she watched us all, a big wide smile, as usual unfazed by the boys. Her white fur clung with static to the leather seat, and her curly white tail slapped in time to some inner rhythm.

"Stevie, I can't pull over, not here, give me a minute. I'll let you out, I promise."

All seven pounds of fluff was hunched on the dashboard, with his tail swishing impatiently. He screeched at me, but softly, worn out by such strong reactions to van life.

The mountain pass took us past Mt. Powell at 13,534 feet with ponderosas and pines thick on either side. The traffic was luckily light on Highway 24 while we were looking for a place to let the pets out to run around. I kept driving, hoping, and then we came around one corner on a downward pass and found one.

With no one behind us it was easy to brake hard and park in the shade of a stand of evergreens. The sun beat down on this June morning. Carefully attaching Stevie to a thin ten-foot rope, I opened the doors. Harold ran for cover, turned his back on us, and let rip. Stevie made a run for it, heading away, away, away from us. The cord flew out of my hand and Stevie ran faster under the cover of shrubs.

"Fuck. Stevie! No, damn it! Don't do this to me! Fuck."

I ran after him and stamped a foot onto the rope, and he bounced backwards. He screamed in frustration, high pitched and furious.

"Now what are you doing to me? Goddammit, I need to go home! I can't stand this, I need to go home…where are we?" He muttered at me, panting at the altitude and stress.

Rosie wandered over, grass sticking out of her mouth, "I don't know but the grass tastes fresher than at home. Try some." She gagged out a mouthful at his feet.

Stevie glared at her, at me, and ran off again. I spent ten minutes chasing him down through the trees, hoping he wouldn't head any deeper into the woods or onto the highway. Trucks passed us with their passengers doing double takes seeing a cat, a rope, and two dogs hidden in the forest. I smiled, waved at surprised faces, and tried to catch the damn cat.

"Please don't do this to me, Stevie. It's better than leaving you at home, right?"

He glared at me. "No." Turning his back on us, he scratched at the dirt. "Can I have some privacy please?"

"Oh, right, sorry." I held onto the rope and looked at the dogs. Harold was still looking none too happy himself because of having a bum tum since he'd left home. At least this time, he got out of the van before the explosions hit. Stevie walked back past me and towards the van.

"You done?"

He kept walking, slowly, panting hard in the heat, his white and grey fur not so helpful in a Northern Colorado summer. With me following, he jumped back into the camper van, sipped at the water, and collapsed. I closed the door quietly and looked for the dogs.

"Anyone hungry?"

Two dogs, one black and one white, raced up, bum tums forgotten, and wagged. They looked at my empty hands. "Yes? You do have a treat, right?"

I opened the van up and pulled out the cooler. Stevie ignored us, exhausted by his own panic attack. Closing the side door again, I handed out lunch, sandwiches for me, pigs' ears for the dogs, and collapsed in the shade, exhausted by the last few days on the road.

What the hell was I thinking? Bringing a cat with us? One who'd only been in a car once to visit a vet as a two month old? A feral foundling who's idea of affection was to latch onto my hand with teeth and claws, not letting go even when hanging upside down. What was I thinking? That it was better than leaving him at home with a neighbor to check on him, that's what. My boy, Stevie, you attack me, bite me, hate me, but you're coming with us. Tough shit, kiddo. Then I burst into tears. Again.

LITTLE STEVIE'S BIG ADVENTURES

STUNNER PASS, COLORADO

Is this what they call a midlife crisis?

The Huffington post describes it as a "dreaded period of time with images of a Harley-mounted silver haired woman riding off into the sunset." Well, that didn't sound too bad to a nomad like me.

Stunner Pass campground is high up in the mountains north of Cumbres, New Mexico, following a well-maintained road for twenty miles to the seasonal village of Platoro. Then though, it suddenly became narrow and winding, with steep drop-offs, and we crossed one 12,000 foot pass after another. To think that those run down rock foundations had been mining encampments blew the cobwebs out of my zoned-out driving mind. Cliff faces had dropped rocks onto National Forest road 250, and it was tricky avoid them while keeping momentum on the gravel and sand. Finally a valley opened up to the left, and crossing the river one last time, I took the fork northwards and pulled into a primitive campground. One other family had set up on the far side under some aspen trees. There was another site nearer the river, high above but close enough to hear it fly by full of snowmelt and timbers.

Looking around nervously, I took a deep breath and simply opened the doors. Out jumped Rosie, then Harold, and finally the Tiger snuck out from under the bed. He stood on the step, sniffed once, looked at the dogs, and then hopped down as if it were just another day.

That evening, sitting at a wooden picnic table next to a raging fire, drinking a glass of malbec, full of curry and good humor, I couldn't help but grin. I'd just had a dramatic shift in lifestyle, that's for sure, quit my job, well, technically it was a three months sabbatical, but we all knew what that meant. I'd bought a van a week before, then packed up my home, left keys with friends, and thrown two dogs and a cat in Van Dreamy and set out for the Northwest. A vague plan, some savings, and a home on wheels, I really couldn't stop grinning. Midlife crisis? Yep. Fine.

Questions and lingering ideas kept spinning round late at night, it's true. What am I doing with my life? Working retail when being self-employed and creative most of my life kept me going nicely? The easy option was no longer so easy. It's not that time is running out, but more along the lines of 'what next?' Time for a challenge apparently. This was it: Taking Cat Stephen for a ride.

Stevie wore his harness reluctantly, hating how the image of a training bra made me snicker. After only a couple of days, there was no more micro-managing the poor bugger. I usually do give up, and even the dogs are rarely on leashes, so why torture the cat? Rosie, the mischief-maker, had taken Stevie the Tiger on a small walkabout. Harold, the biggest and best dog in the world, lay on his blanket near the van, watching us all. He weighed in at sixty-five pounds, a solid mid-sized black dog with a white chest and front paws. His tail stood at half-mast most of the time unless he sensed a threat, then chest filled and tail raised a challenge to the incomers. In reality, he wore a transparent sign telling other dogs to attack him.

Is this is a mid-life crisis? Leaving home, no real plans, no real goals? Buying new toys, that is, vehicles? Big changes? Yes, probably. I've been restless for a long time. It's not new for me to travel loosely. Or to take little backcountry camping trips. For three months though? No, I haven't done that for more than a decade. Not since I'd packed up my home in Madrid, NM, and moved to San Francisco and then Alaska. I'd had nothing going on so why not eh? This time, the job was good enough, great co-workers who'd become friends, some good customers, some idiots, but it was retail. Indoors. I'm an outdoor dog. Working under fluorescent lights for eight hours a day, answering stupid questions, that's what was draining. My joie de vivre, curiosity, and interest in people and their stories took a hike for a few years.

"Ah, but, you're ALONE in the middle of the San Juan Mountains, that's not going to help is it?" Harold is so pedantic.

Yes, it is. Time out from having to make small talk. Time out from routines. Time with the critters in beautiful places to recharge my inner batteries, well, yes that will help. Help work out what next. Where next. Turning fifty next year, a concept that doesn't exactly freak me out, but it gives pause. Time to see if this is how I want to spend the next ten years. Is it? In the meantime, there was a job to do. An outdoor kind of a job. "Anyone hungry?"

Harold jumped up and ran to the campervan with tail wagging high. Rosie pushed her way to the front of the line, normal behavior for the middle 'child'. Stevie hopped onto the wooden table and stood next to the cooler. I doled out the dinners, and settled back to watching a fire with a wine in hand. Brain quietened. Smile broadened. Critters munched. Not a bad start.

"I'm sorry. I'm sorry Harold. I didn't know that looking out the window in the middle of the night and growling meant your bum was about to explode."

I picked up the cat, opened the door, and threw out the dog. I dropped the cat. Looked for a flashlight, turned it on and checked out the damage. Stevie stared at me from the bed. Rosie curled up on my pillow. Crap. Everywhere. One big boy bum tum on the rugs, carpet and dog bed, all around the edges as if he'd tried to be tidy as it flew out. Poor bugger. One foot stood in a sludge pile. Grab cat, throw out rugs and bed, take the water bowl, and step outside, drop the cat back inside and close the door. Damn. Damn. Damn. A midnight crisis was not a good start. A shitty start you could say...

Harold whimpered most of the night. Despite the wish to leave him outside, just in case, but with a frost on the grass, the threat of bears, and an overwhelming guilt, I let him back onto my bed. He fell fast asleep. I didn't.

With the fire going and a brisk fog surrounding us, it was most definitely springtime in the mountains with a lingering blue-grey mist down in the valley. Harold ate his breakfast as if nothing had happened. Stevie followed Rosie into the trees around the van. I pulled out bedding, carpet, rugs, clothes, crates, pretty much everything. Since I had to clean thoroughly this morning, it was a perfect time to reorganize. Note to self: Don't just make packing lists - use them. The number of odds and ends forgotten was growing in number so out came the notepad for another list.

The aspens were only just budding out, and a slight light green hue covered the hills around us. To either side of the narrow valley, mountains rose to over 10,000 feet, an alpine profile of boulders and bare land, with a few grey white slashes of snow in the south facing creek beds. Lower down a forest began; thick mixed conifers were home to much wildlife and the morning alarm of birdsong echoed around our meadow.

With coffee in hand, it was time to look at maps, brush teeth, and build a new routine. With the critters, and for me too, it really helps to have some kind of routine, otherwise Harold stares at me constantly, uncertain and is a right nervous Nellie. That first morning started us off with a pattern of fire, coffee, food, and a short walk including Little Stevie. Back to the van, throw the cat in the van, and then a mile or so hike with two happy dogs and one hyper human, caffeined and ready to explore.

Stunner Pass was a miners' camp in 1892 during the Colorado Gold Rush. Over four hundred miners lived and worked up there and the foundations of a few shacks remained. How they took the gold back down to the nearest town, or brought supplies up here astounded me: horseback and carts in snow and rain, what a combination. The Post Office even delivered mail by sled dog teams. Most of the miners left in search of more gold and the encampment faded away as another dream took hold.

I took buckets down to the Alamosa River and filled up enough for washing myself, two dog bowls, and rinsing out the last of Harold's poopy butt mess. Our picnic table was covered with blankets, clothes, and kitchen supplies, all taking up space. Not the time for writing, perhaps a nap then? Yep, a nap, good idea. With all the critters inside, doors closed, we settled down for an eleven o'clock nap.

SALIDA, COLORADO

A few days alone in the mountains did wonders for my confidence. We can do this. It's not so bad, right? I talked to the pets constantly; full of words now that Trader Joes didn't use them all up on customer service. Harold followed me with his eyes, Rosie lay at my feet, and Stevie watched from under the van. I packed up the last of the kitchen crates and stowed them under the bed. We had time for a last hike with the pups before we drove to Salida to visit friends.

Mornings were bright and crisp, and I was glad to have the insulated coveralls with me, a last minute addition that had made Katie and Peter laugh. "It's summer, you know." Luckily peer pressure doesn't work on me, I'd even packed snow boots just to be sure. Perfect on mornings like those at 11, 561 feet.

Salida appeals more in theory than reality, like Taos does for me. I always want to visit, and usually make it up there once a year, but once parked by the river, I usually don't know what to do with myself. That time was no different. Britney and AJ had invited me to stay, I knew where they lived in an A-frame cabin, but instead I walked around downtown with the dogs, popped into a pet store and bought treats for all, and then stopped for lunch at my favorite place, the Riverside pub. A burger and beer for me, treats for Harold and Rosie, life was good. Yet I worried about Stevie in the van. Was it too hot in the sunshine? Had I left windows open enough for air but not big enough for a little furry body to climb out of? I finished the burger, paid up, and headed back to find Stevie fast asleep under the bed again.

Salida has spread over recent years, but downtown is still historical with tall brick buildings a hundred years old, with a thriving business in tourism and art.

Salida was settled in 1880 by the Denver and Rio Grande Railroad and became a hub for mining and agriculture. These days it's known for the outdoor activities, what with the Arkansas River, rafting, kayaking, and even skiing near by, but I did nowt. The post office has been here since 1881, but I sent no postcards. Instead, I drove off, getting lost briefly in the downtown streets before heading east three miles to a BLM campground. Well, it was free, but busy with what looked like long-term campers, all stared at me territorially as I drove by and parked near the river. Dogs barked at us, campers glared, the river was fast and rough, and so no, I'd not go back. Emergencies yes, but to relax? Nope. It was too much of a contrast after the peace of Stunner Pass and Platoro. Stevie was grounded for his own safety and that didn't go over well. The dogs were tied up, and I hid inside, waiting for morning so we could head north. I drank too many beers, peed in a bucket, spilt pee on that damn rug, and worried about Harold, Rosie, and Stevie.

Why was I doing this? Why had I brought them with me? Well, what else would I have done? Paid a house sitter? Then I couldn't have afforded such a trip. Plus, I was checking out places we could move to, as a family. The only way I ever really know if a place is pet-friendly is when I show up with dogs and in this case, a cat. Salida was very dog friendly; the waitress brought them treats and water, checked on the pups more than on me, and everywhere we'd walked, hands had reached for furry ears. So yes, Salida was pet friendly but could I see myself living there? No. I don't want to work in the service industry, dependent on tips and seasonal work. Okay, time to move on. But what about Britney and AJ, why didn't I visit? I don't know. I just didn't.

BEARS

If I'm going to be mauled, bitten, and/or killed I have a choice of Black Bear and the Grizzly. I'm not sure which is better. The Black Bear is smaller, weighing in at only 650 #s maximum, it lives all over the damn place, and last I read that there were over 600,000 in the States. The statistics are meant to make me happier, help me relax but knowing that there have been on average 25 bear attacks per year doesn't actually make me feel any better. Maybe because the advice given is vague and contradictory. I'd like someone to give me a definitive answer as to what to do. Stand tall and make noise? Climb a tree? Stare down or fall down? I'm more likely to shit myself and freeze.

Grizzlies, now there's a bear worth running from,

although you don't really want to run. But wouldn't you? Facing a bear, wouldn't you just want to run away? Grizzlies, topping over 1200 #s with a hump on their shoulders, should be easily recognizable, right? But a bear is a bear is a bear. I have the spray from REI but can't say that helps me. It's the uncertainty. Knowing that an attack might happen, but then again they might just stare at me and amble off. What happened if one decides that Little Stevie looks like a dunkin donut? What would I do? What would the dogs do? Well, those questions kept me awake at night. In my sleep, a grizzly stares me down, I back off slowly, asking myself, am I meant to climb a tree or play dead? A black bear though, they like it when you lie still, so much easier to chew.

Years ago, when I first came to the States, I ended up at a Rainbow Gathering in Minnesota in July. Peace, love, sex, drugs, and the munchies. I fell asleep (passed out) in a tent one night after getting the munchies, the food storage tent that is, kind of like a 7-11 in the woods. Clashing pans, yelling, screaming, stomping, I woke suddenly, lying on the dirt floor with a bag of half-eaten chips next to me. A big, and I mean big silhouette stood in the tent's opening then turned and ran into the night.

A black bear, yes, with me in a tent with enough

food for a few hundred people. I finished the chips and stumbled off looking for my own tent. If only I could remember which one it was.

CROSHO LAKE, COLORADO

Stevie fought me, fought the leash, van, screens, and even Rosie. All claws and energy, he flew around the van, yowling and scratching anything in his way. The lake campground was empty but for two men in their sixties, fishermen and friendly. I'd set up camp near the trees with a fire going and dinner on. But I couldn't relax, my instinct said to leave, to keep driving, but I didn't have it in me. My head kept me awake at night, worrying about the critters, questioning my life and throwing out too many ideas as to what I should, should, and really should do next. I was worn down, bursting into tears, and completely on edge.

I closed the door behind me, whistled for the pups, and took off for a hike. Exercise to wear me out was the plan of action, to stop me thinking and get back into my body. The lake was some thirty acres, small and surrounded by trees both deciduous and evergreen. It was beautiful but I didn't like it. The saving grace was a five by twenty foot snow bank. Yes, a three-foot high snow bank slowly melted next to the van, dogs digging happily for hours at a time. One redeeming factor for a shitty day.

In Yampa, on the last leg of the day I'd stopped for supplies. Mrs. Montgomery's Store filled my cooler with cheese, cream, and beer for the night ahead. Mrs. M herself, five foot nothing, thick grey hair in a bun, and a wide toothy smile, gave me a map of directions to this lake, saying it was easier than explaining since the road got so narrow that no one ever believed her! A sweet old woman, she and her husband had run the business for over forty years, and the shelves were full of hardware, clothes, camping and hunting gear, canned meat, cheap cookies, soda, chips, postcards, hats, sunscreen and fishing supplies. The beer was crap though but heh, it was better than nothing given how exhausted I was.

Deciding to give up my job, to travel for months in a van I hardly knew, with three animals dependent on me, all because of some inner restlessness, my energy lagged. Oh well, we're here now. Crosho Lake is one deep (175 foot!) mostly spring fed mountain lake and access is by 4x4 roads, not that I knew that as I was driving there. Mrs. M hadn't mentioned that fact. It was beautiful though, and yes, walking helped me. At least it helped the pups stretch their legs. Stunner Pass felt safe.

Crosho didn't. I don't know why. Nothing happened,
but I didn't relax there. Neither did Stevie. I let him out
but with a light, long rope attached to him. He took off
into the trees. The dogs followed him. I stumbled after
him, dropping my coffee as I ducked under branches
and climbed over tree stumps. He headed straight uphill,
higher, faster, and getting away from me, from the van.
I kept up, pulling him back every now and again. It was
only when the forest ran out and a gravel road greeted
him that Stevie stopped. He stared. Then he backed
down to the van and jumped inside, hiding under the
bed. I tied his rope to the door and left it open as I went
looking for my coffee mug.

VAN DREAMY

"I like yours better!" I'd joked.

Terry grinned at me, "We'd better not tell him
though. Just pretend we haven't talked, okay?"

Terry was in his seventies, a long term Santa Fean, an
artist, and he too was looking for a van to convert for
long travels. He was shorter than me at 5 ft. 5 to my 5
ft. 8. Wiry, tanned and very much a local in style, a
desert rat by the local vernacular, we'd met on Old Las
Vegas Highway by chance, checking out a Ford van for

sale. While waiting for the owner to arrive Terry and I had started chatting easily and freely. I was in the '95 4Runner, a worn out yet reliable dark green SUV with the dogs in the back, tongues hanging out. Terry was in a 2003 Dodge Conversion van, grey and red, clean as a whistle, and just about right for me and mine.

Hmm…I'd made the joke about buying his van instead of the Ford for sale, same price. Terry laughed, opened it up, and said, "Deal!"

Simple as that. We'd both chatted to the owner of the Ford, made our excuses for not buying it, and then subtly exchanged phone numbers. Back at home, with a little research, I'd found out that the Dodge van was worth almost twice what I'd offered. I called Terry to say it didn't feel right.

"Well, I talked to Mary, my daughter, and she said it's okay. We'd prefer to think of you traveling in our van and not the 4Runner, you can't camp in that for three months!" He insisted. And here we are, only a few weeks later, living out of Motel Vera Danell Van Dreamy McLeamy.

With not the time to do much of anything, I just folded down the back bench seat to make a bed, took out one of the passenger seats by the side door, threw in the bedding and blankets. Under the bed from the side door, I stashed crates of kitchen gear, a cooler, water, and pet food. The clothes filled the shelf above the back door. In the passenger's foot well went the boots and winter gear. From the back door, more storage under the bed, which filled up fast with camping gear like firewood, newspapers, tarps, and tools. Yep, we were ready. Three nights before leaving for the Northwest, we'd all slept in there, the dogs and cat and myself, outside my home in New Mexico. I even fed everyone in there and took naps in the afternoons. They all loved it. At the time, even Stevie loved it.

STEAMBOAT SPRINGS, COLORADO

"I need help."

"Oh. Okay." The woman behind the counter looked nervously at her co-worker then checked me out, noting dirty jeans, wild unbrushed hair, and startled eyes. She took another look outside and saw Rosie and Harold in the front seats of the van, watching us. Stevie popped up onto the dashboard and the woman laughed in delight. She turned back to me, pushing reading glasses high on her forehead. "How can I help, dear?"

Relaxing, I told of Stevie's panic attacks, the dogs' messy bums, and my anxiety over the whole trip.

"Well, yes, that is a lot to take care of, isn't it?

Let's see. I have Rescue Remedy, do you know this product?" At my nodding smile, she opened it and passed it over. "Have some now while we go through the list." She had a no-nonsense air about her, solid and unflustered by my obvious distress. She strode to an aisle in the far corner and picked through the full shelves. Ten drops on my tongue and then I followed Susan around the pet store, a high-end pet store. The prices made me nervous but this is what a credit card is for, right? Emergencies. She compiled a stack of odds and ends for the stomach problems, and suggested feeding the dogs rice for a few days to ease the stress, adding chicken broth for flavor.

"This though is what we really need, isn't it?" She passed me something called Calming Treats. Valerian for dogs. Yes, perfect, but I wondered about how it would be for a cat. He's so small.

Susan met me back at the counter and called the company to find out, nodding her head and explaining the situation. "Okay, that's great, thank you so much, dear. Yes, that is fine. Thank you again." Smiling she rang up the total, I handed the card over as she told me to just give Little Stevie a quarter dose at a time. Not too much, all right?

Susan then chatted about the area, telling me to drive to Steamboat Reservoir, not that I did, but she confirmed the route to the National Forest camping near the Mt Zirkel Wilderness north of town. "You just missed a big event yesterday, the mountain bike ride from the lake into town, all down hill, you can imagine how fast some of them were going! Incredible. My husband and I live near Clark, have you heard of it? There's an old General Store you have to visit, and that's all I'm saying!" Her easy smile gave me confidence to keep going.

In the van, I gave out treats. Stevie got a full size helping though, no half measures at this point. We sat there for a moment and then my phone beeped at me. Surprised, I saw it was a message from my brother in England.

"There's a liquor store next to that pet store, you'd better stock up!"

Damn technology! I'd set up a GPS tracker for my family to keep an eye out and to follow along. I didn't really expect Pete to be that on top of it. I texted back asking what kind of beer, to which he replied, 'a local lager please'. Not to disappoint, I carried the tracker with me and bought us a six-pack and dark chocolate.

Opening the van door, no one pushed past me, trying to get out. Harold lay on the bed in the back, his tail slowly wagging. Rosie was curled up on my driver's seat, smiling and drooling. Stevie? Stevie was on the top shelf, legs draped over the edge, his eyes glazed and loudly purring. Is Valerian like heroin for critters?

Susan waved from the pet store door in her bright green shorts and yellow sweatshirt looking very much like an outdoor hiker. If only I'd bought a case of those calming treats: It would have helped in Washington. Well, I didn't but in the van with sleepy animals sprawled everywhere I relaxed, started the engine, and headed into the hills once more.

At the stop sign, the road forked north on County Road 129 towards the reservoir. Clark, Colorado, was a small town twenty miles or so up into the mountains that had been a former mining town next to Hahn's Peak. The General Store had a huge sign announcing Ice Cream! A wide wooden deck wrapped around the old western building and it was easy to picture how it might have been a hundred years ago during the Gold Rush. Traveling through the Rockies kept bringing me to rural little villages and settlements far off the beaten track, full of a local rich history, tales of hard working restless families mining the land, hoping for a better life, taking on the winters and lack of an easy life because of this need to explore. Hmm…my version was so much easier.

The store was full, with even a small library and

post office in the left side of the open plan building. I checked out a few books, and dropped off another I'd just finished. The shelves in the grocery section had the basics, cans, water, camping needs, and some beer and wine. With a basket of eggs, tortillas, water, beer, and dog treats, I asked about the ice cream.

"Oh, you just missed Earl. He'll be back tomorrow though, most days really, although it's a little pre-season right now. Earl, yep, he's a reliable sort, been here most of his life, not like me, I come and go, spend my winters in Arizona, who can blame me? That'll be $20.54 please. Cash? Oh yes, cash is always better isn't it, that's what I tell my missus, that we should just live off cash, it comes and goes that's for sure but I like to know what's in my wallet and there's no other way to keep track is there, anything else?"

He took a breath. I shook my head.

At Glen Eden, the national forest road on the right followed Elk River as Susan had told me. Another ten miles and signs pointed across a field and down a loop of a rough dirt track. Slowly the van bumped and bounced over the rocks and dips, it was only a quarter mile but slow-going all the same. The river raced past, slightly below and to the right of us. Pulling off, the flat area under a few fifty-foot ponderosas became home for a few days. It's always tempting to keep going, maybe, maybe that next campsite is better, nicer, something that this one isn't. This trip though, my need to keep looking evaporated within a few days and that first spot was always just fine thank you very much.

With only a few other vehicles up and down this track, the wind and the raging river were the only sounds. Doors open, all my dopey critters jumped out, even Stevie, the new junkie. He glanced around, unconcerned at the new environment and yawned. Big stretch, and off he wandered. "Cool man, this is cool. Oh wow, look at those huge trees. Just wait, I'm going to climb those trees some day, not right now, but I will, some day."

Rosie disappeared down the riverbank and I had a moment's panic that the river would wash her away. Jeez, can't I ever relax? Stop worrying about the animals? Nope. At home, I worried about the neighborhood dogs that'd killed another dog this spring. In the mountains, the fear was about bears. Here the river. In towns, it was the heat, or traffic, or or or... Fuck it. Relax will you? It was time for a beer. Think of your big brother instead.

Not sure what to do with myself, my afternoon passed by with a mix of books, beer, stretching, naps, eating, keeping a campfire going, and then looking for more firewood. The National Forest folks had obviously been busy here as along Elk River lay dead and down cottonwoods and ponderosas, the trunks were too long for me to use but with enough smaller branches to break and carry. The campfire ticked along nicely, a good thing as the cloud cover was becoming dark, heavy, and the very real threat of snow made me nervous. I pulled out all the bedding, and reworked my bed first, with the sleeping bag opened as another layer, and with dog blankets spread on the floor for extra insulation. Glad for the coveralls once again, I prepped for a cold night ahead.

The valley was perhaps a quarter mile wide with steep mountains on three sides, thick with ponderosas and pines, a narrow footpath lead us up high overlooking the river and campers below. Horses, deer, and elk tracks had worn out a zigzag path over the boulders and through the trees. Why hadn't I brought the bear spray though? Hiking in coveralls, a hat, snow boots and a camera wasn't exactly practical of me. I kept to the edges of the deeper forest, checking for bear, calling the dogs, and glad Stevie was locked inside Van Dreamy. The wind kicked up and clouds raced overhead, gathering over Little Agnes Mountain to the northwest, one that reached 11,495 feet all told. Looking back, the cottonwoods lined Elk River heading southwest, the national forest road following it around curves, homesteads, and out of sight. Smoke from a ranch reassured me that we weren't lonely as much as solitary by choice. I stumbled around nervously, watching the sky darkening, yet smiling at a glimpse of the van stuck between two towering pines. Rosie bound up, her usual wide smile and curly tail beating to the rhythm of her steps. She sniffed and peed on everything, sticking close for once. That made me nervous. Again.

"Harold? Harold? Come on boy, let's go."

Nothing, no sound of collar and tags, no sight of a black and white boy in the trees.

"Who's hungry?" I yelled and took the direct route back down the ledge towards the valley. Jingle, jingle, yep, works every time, Harold jumped up on the rock behind me, tongue out, tail waving.

"Come on then, you did say hungry, didn't you? I'm starving. Again." He bounced down the hillside at full speed with me stumbling behind.

Tucked up for the night, full bellies all around, we assumed our positions. Rosie, on the blanket on the floor. Harold in the driver's seat. Stevie on his shelf. All was quiet and calm. Another good night ahead. Or so I thought.

"What was that?"

Stevie growled his little tiger warning and his tail swished in anger as he stared out the back window. A glow from another campfire lit up the far end of the valley, loud voices, men's voices, yelling and howling in the pitch black. Harold jumped onto the bed next to Stevie and the boys lay with hackles up, growling together. I sat up, grabbed a flashlight and thought about exploring, then thought again and locked the doors. Yelling, loud, and drunk, the boys' singing echoed down the canyon, waking Rosie too. She climbed into the front seat, staring the wrong way. Thoughts of pack mentality and mayhem kept me awake. I checked the locked doors and windows, with keys next to me. The GPS tracker I'd mentioned earlier has a panic button, an emergency response message for if ever I'd broken a leg, been seriously hurt, for those life-threatening events. It would send out the call and location, but it had to be serious. For some reason, that night at Elk River, I was scared. Seriously scared. On the floor next to the door were the bear spray and a knife. The flashlight strapped to both for a quick grab. My phone on and ready to call for help.

I didn't sleep. Rosie did. As did the boys.

In the morning, I made another campfire and strong

coffee, not in the best of moods. The critters wandered around, keeping clear of me, even Rosie stopped herself from the normal licking frenzy she usually greets me with each day. She wagged cautiously from ten feet away. Snow covered the peaks but the sky had cleared to a crisp cold blue. The coffee warmed me, a fire warmed me, and finally the sun topped the hills around us. Stevie back in the van, we took off, with the bear spray this time.

As we headed off up the road to explore around that next corner, smiling faces greeted me from a circle of three tents. Six of them, all twenty-somethings in REI jackets like mine, offered me coffee and apologies if they'd kept me up last night. "Finished school, see? We had to celebrate before Chuck heads off to Cali, right?" Laughter and stories of classes skipped, plans for summer, and treats for the dogs, we chatted a while. Embarrassed at my fears, I kept quiet, pretended I hadn't heard a thing. And then I made an escape for the hills.

What is it about Bears, and yes, I capitalize it because that's how I say it, okay?

Bear Country. Be Bear Aware:

- Don't surprise bears: make noise. (Am I meant to talk outloud to myself?)

- Keep a clean camp. Hang food in a tree or store in a vehicle. (But I sleep in the van.)
- Dogs antagonize bears. Keep them leashed. (Tell them that. And what about cats?)

Well, why am I so scared of them this trip? I'm in a van, safe, well, mostly. But all the warnings of bears and cougars kept me on edge as we hiked each day, miles at a time, checking on the dogs constantly, worrying about whether to put the food in the van or not. What am I meant to do?

Last year, camping in the San Juan Mountains with three dogs, yes, I had three dogs for quite a while, we were living out of the back of an old 4Runner. In a small clearing, I'd made a fire, had dinner, and was relaxing nicely with a book and a beer. You see where this is going, don't you? The dogs were all lying around my feet, fast asleep, tired after hiking around Williams Creek Reservoir. Slowly, one by one, the dogs got up and walked quietly over to the truck. Harold and Rosie jumped up, stepping over the bed made up in the back, and claimed the front seats. They stared out the front window, away from me. All around me, the dense pine forest was a mass of dark underbrush and small creeks. Oliver, the third dog, a miniature Great Dane in shape if not reality, followed the others, but he lay on the bed, staring at me and softly got my attention.

"Woof, woof, please listen to me, woof."

Behind me, heavy breathing and solid footsteps came closer. I slowly picked up the beer, holding my book, and stepped briskly over to the truck, shut the tailgate and closed the window before climbing in a side door. All doors locked.

Oliver gave me a grateful lick and fell asleep. I sat up, reading and sipping the last of the beer but never did see what was loitering in those trees.

SARATOGA, WYOMING

"Well, he would, wouldn't he? Him being white and me black, it's only natural that he likes a pint of porter!" Jasmine poured me another. She was a young city girl from San Diego with a short tight afro, big smile, and clothes you don't often see in a rural town like Saratoga, all tight denim and flash jewelry. She wore it well. "And I like white chocolate, so we're doing great! That's four dollars please. Where did you say you're from?"

Yes, she was bored. I was the only customer in the brewery sitting at the bar. Me, I

It wasn't boredom more about needing to use my vocal chords for more than simply asking, *anyone hungry*? A little croaky to start but soon we were chatting away. She told me how her and Jeff work in San Diego over winters and then look for seasonal work in different states for the summers. She'd worked in Jackson Hole, Memphis, Flagstaff, and even Tampa. He'd met her in Memphis. They'd traveled ever since yet she didn't think of herself as a traveler. It's a lifestyle for me; it's an attitude and curiosity. For her it was work pure and simple, an economic drive.

Jasmine leaned against the counter and half-heartedly wiped glasses whenever the boss wandered in to check on us. Me the forty-nine year old and this twenty-three year old laughed up a storm, outbidding each other with the strange things customers ask in retail. Her experience was mostly behind a bar and mine recently at Trader Joes in Santa Fe.

"I forget that I have an accent, you know," and admitted to getting annoyed by the tourists welcoming me to Santa Fe, when I'd lived there on and off for over twenty years. "One woman asked where I was from so I said Maine. Oh, wrong thing to say. She started asking where exactly, and so I mentioned a small town on an island I knew: Sunset, Deer Isle. The sale finished, and this customer turned to the next in line, 'Sarah here is from Maine, isn't that interesting?' The next woman in line answered, 'Oh really? I am too.' Busted!"

Jasmine laughed and told of the old geezers in this white little cowboy town finding her fascinating, asking about her hair, suntans, religion and then asking her out. She found it funny but no, didn't plan on coming back.

I did though. I loved it here, well, for a visit I did. We'd driven up from Steamboat over snow-capped mountain passes, along small curvaceous highways, and into an open high valley leading into Wyoming. The state sign stood in a parking area on a windy bluff and I'd pulled over. No traffic around so with Stevie on his rope, I'd let everyone out, taken a silly amount of photos of the dogs peeing on the sign and Stevie watching them from the van. Good times. Good times.

Finding a free campsite hadn't been too difficult. The problem was that the campground was completely flooded, to the point where Stevie wouldn't/ couldn't get out of the van. I'd taken off my boots, rolled up the jeans, and followed the pups bouncing through the North Platte River. The snowmelt that season had wiped out all the parking area, trashcans, tables, and surrounded one toilet. The mozzies found us fast and I quickly hopped back into the van, closing the windows ands screens pretty quickish. So much for that campground, thanks BLM.

Backtracking to Saratoga, the city offered it's own camping next to a small reservoir. Perfectly empty, wide open, spacious, and yes, we camped there for a few days. I'd found a spot at the far end, one where there was no reason to drive by yet still close enough to some vault toilets, with our own little sandy beach, fire pit and a wooden picnic table. For seven dollars a night and safe for all the critters, I relaxed completely. Finally.

Saratoga was a fascinating little break for me. Town itself has two branches of the North Platte River passing through, flooding the parks and some back yards, with sandbags lining streets and homes. The population hovers around 1693, increasing with the hunting season apparently. Hearing of the free Hobo Hot Springs downtown, I'd parked in the shade of some huge cottonwoods and elms along the river and crossed the bridge to the springs. The city had built them up with a good sized brick building for bathrooms and showers, as well as bricking in a swimming pool sized hot spring with steps, a ramp, seating area, and a short maintained path to the cold river racing past. All for free! I couldn't believe my luck and lay in the sun, soaked in the shade, thoroughly washed hair and body in the showers, and slowly made my way back to the van. The critters slept on the bed, and barely moved when I returned each afternoon. This was one new routine I embraced. Soak, nap, walk to brewery, head back to camp, make a fire, read and write. The dogs and I explored the lake, scaring up so many ducks and heron that Harold didn't know which way to run. Stevie even came with us in the mornings much to his delight. He'd race ahead of me, catch up with Rosie and then jump on Harold, scaring the poor big boy, and then race back to rub against my legs as I stretched.

Wandering around town during the days didn't delight me as much as the springs or brewery, but happily enough a library allowed me to sit and write and check all my emails, blogs and websites to send off the latest articles on traveling with pets. Yep, business taken care of, we'd hang out at the lake again, doing nothing and quite happily so.

STEVIE

"You will take him, right? I can't leave him at the shelter. My dogs would kill him." My neighbor waited for the sigh and unexpected response of "yes, bring him over."

Mo turned up the next afternoon with a cat carrier, bowls, wet food, and the smallest and scruffiest little kitten staring out at us. All white fluff and squinty eyes, it sat in the back of the carrier. In the kitchen with the dogs stuck in the living room, Mo handed me the fur ball.

"I found him in a wood pile at work, heard this meowing all high pitched and scared. There she was, well, I thought it was a girl but it's a boy. You don't mind, do you? The vets checked him out last night, he's good to go, and they'll fix him for you for free in a couple of months."

Mo stopped talking nervously as I held a tiny kitten in one hand. He stared up at me, did this tiny bugger. It was love at first sight. How could I do anything but smile? I held him to my neck and cuddled him until a soft purr vibrated against my skin.

"He's under a pound in weight, it's amazing he made it out there. Want a cup of tea? You sit down, I'll make it." She made us sit at the table while making tea for us both. Nestling a feral kitten to me, I leaned back and sipped at a mug of chamomile. The propane heater kicked in, a roar of heat in my little kitchen telling me of the chill in the air. Outside the temperature dropped. It was a cold November night with a freezing wind and a threat of snow. Thinking of this little fella in a woodpile in this weather broke my heart.

"Little Stevie, you're staying with us."

ATLANTIC CITY, WYOMING

I'd heard of it, but had no idea why. It popped up on my maps and recognizing the name, I figured why not? It's not like I had real commitments to be anywhere except in Washington at the Northwest Overland Rally in a few weeks. Surely I'd make it by then? Although I'd only just got out of Colorado and that had taken more than ten days. Oh well. Slow and steady as my gran used to tell us.

The road to Atlantic City took us slightly on another detour, a roundabout way to get to Jackson Hole, a place on the list to visit for some reason. It wasn't so much the National Parks but something else, and once again, no details stuck in mind. I'd done too much research over winter and taken too few notes apparently. A small sign pointed south and left and we turned onto a wide gravel road across rangeland. Nothing in sight even at this open elevation of over 7,200 feet, but by the looks of it a river flowed somewhere in the hills. Ah, Rock Creek feeds enough water for the town's trees in the valley below the Antelope Hills. Once again, I wonder how often have I crossed the Continental Divide? Up and down all the bloody time. I was over the Rockies. Done, that is.

Atlantic City was another mining town, once thriving, then abandoned, and now growing again as a tourist destination and home for those looking to live in a small unique community. Rather like Madrid, NM, my home in the States. A grocery store, a pub, a diner, and a small volunteer fire station. The population sign announced 57 inhabitants. I could believe it. It had been a booming gold mining settlement, another in the tale of the restless fortune seekers. What drove them onwards and what kept some staying despite dwindling benefits? The tavern drew me but after sticking my head in and seeing how dark and depressing it was, we drove on, looking for a campsite for the night. Dispersed camping on BLM property surrounded the settlement, but with dense trees, a threat of hungry bears, and swampy dirt tracks, I kept on driving. The road climbed uphill again, into the rangeland with huge views, no trees, and nowhere for bears to loiter as they assessed my little furry family. Perfect. I pulled over, parked, let the critters out and started making dinner. No campfires, much too windy, and I missed the comfort of the flames. The dogs ran up to the hilltop and barked. Uh oh. Where's the cat? Grab cat. ("Oy!") Open van. Drop cat. Close van. Check on dogs. It's a process. One I'm getting used to.

Rosie's bum stuck out of a deep hole. Harold lay in

another, huffing and puffing madly.

"What the hell are you two doing?"

"Squirrel!"

Harold looked up, shook his nose free of dirt, and dove back in. I yelled at Rosie and her tail wagged furiously, but didn't even look at me.

"Yep, squirrels! Amazing, they just look like dinner to me…go on, don't worry about us, and go get a beer! We'll be right here, won't we, Harry?"

The clouds built up and the temperature dropped fast as the evening wore on. The dogs lay at my feet, finally admitting defeat, and I'd fed them the usual kibble, pills, and chicken broth. Stevie had joined us outside, watching the wild birds zipping across the grasses as he asked questions. "What's that Hawold? Can I chase it?"

"I wouldn't, it's a hawk. Best go underneath the van, kiddo. I'll tell you when it's gone." Harold sat tall, chest out, taking on the job of protector.

It was an easy evening for all of us, and even hyper Rosie slept on the stunted grass at my feet uncomplaining. The beer had gone down nicely too. I was happy. Relaxed. No bears here.

A truck pulled up and stopped next to us in the morning. I'd just made coffee, the critters were out and about, sniffing and peeing as they do. I grabbed my jacket and wandered over.

"Hi, I'm Dave, just thought I'd say hello." He was a tall thickset man in his sixties, with a tidy short grey beard and dark brown eyes half hidden by the cowboy hat. He shook hands with me and declined coffee. "I wanted to see if that bear bothered you last night?"

"Bear?"

"Yup. I was asleep in the front of the truck. I'm damn glad I didn't set up my tent. Smelly fella he was, big by the sounds of it, all heavy steps and deep breathing? You didn't smell him then? That's what woke me up. Damn bears, they're everywhere."

PINEDALE, WYOMING

Parked in the shade beside the Tourist Information Center one afternoon, I craved conversation again. What's happening to me? I don't like people, do I? Or was it just Trader Joes that silenced me? Am I recovering? Ah, Trader Joes, where customers stand and ask, "where is the cheese?" I'd point and smile. "Under the four by ten foot sign that says Cheese." At which point came the inevitable, "Oh what a nice accent. Welcome to America!"

I'm amazed I didn't get into more trouble than I did. The accent though, strangers don't listen to my words, just get stuck on that foreign accent of mine, a mix of English and New Mexican at this point. I can talk of being deported, or stuck in Tijuana without a visa and money, and all they hear is blah blah queen blah teatime blah. This then is I why I write, to get the stories out regardless. That day in Pinedale though, I needed conversation, anything really, even about the weather.

"Lovely weather isn't it, dear?" said the small tidy woman behind the counter, peering over her glasses at me. "It's a bit dry and we're worried about the fire season, but I say make hay while the sun shines, don't you?" She smiled up at me and reached for a stack of maps and leaflets. "You look like you camp, you do, don't you dear?"

I nodded and started to speak when she interrupted me with a detailed description of the numerous campgrounds in the area, adding another map for Jackson Hole and the Tetons.

"You'll love it, but the dogs, they don't like dogs in those parks you know? Did your pups need water? Let's go get some, shall we? I have a bucket out the backdoor, come along dear, and do keep up."

I never did get a word in and so once dogs were watered, we took a wander around town. I'd

deliberately stopped here as a friend, Josh, had spent
summers here with his dad when he was a kid. Pinedale
nowadays is a bit of a tourist trap for kayaking, hunting
and other such manly outdoor pursuits. The population
hovers around 2,050 but dips and climbs depending on
the seasons. The main strip followed Highway 191
north, and local businesses lined each side, not the usual
tourist stuff, but a mix of real general stores with cafes,
diners, and clothing and hunting places. Wandering off
the main loop, I came across a small box, 'Free
Library'. Perfect, pulling out my glasses, I picked a
couple of no-brainer murder mysteries and happily
ambled back to the van. With pups and Stevie inside
and under shade, I headed over to a brewpub. Well, it
was cocktail hour somewhere, right? And I needed to
study my maps. Maybe even talk to someone?

Greg and Sheila joined me at the bar. Greg was
around my age, a red head, weathered outdoorsman,
who talked of construction jobs taking him all over the
state. His girlfriend was skinny, wiry like a speed freak,
and not surprisingly full of energy. They both asked
many questions about the accent, and ignoring my
desire to curl up and read a book, I talked of Europe, of
New Mexico, and this camping trip. They talked of
work, her in an office where he's a crew boss, and how
they met a year ago, and how he's fixing up her house

in Lander, but her teenage kid doesn't like him.

"We take off when he goes to his dad's, thought we'd stay here in the motel down the road tonight."

"The stress of dating at our age," she laughed, as if I'd know what she meant.

JACKSON HOLE, WYOMING

Snake River Brewery, on a Sunday afternoon, it was packed, loud, horrible, and yet exactly what was needed. Sitting between Dave and Frank in this two-storied warehouse restaurant, I watched the television, ordered a Rolling Thunder, which is a German style lager and very good I must say.

"Have you read any good books recently?" His baldhead shone under the fluorescent lights as he introduced himself. His hands were clean, manicured, an indoor dog, and his smile was open and so we shook hands. He was nice, his hands, his shirt, his smile were all nice. Not my type at all but I'd been quiet for a few weeks and needed attention, not fussy at that point. He nodded at the notebook in my lap.

"I saw you making notes, and I thought maybe she's a writer, you know, a travel writer. I couldn't help but wonder. Are you writing about Jackson?" He sipped his beer and carried on. "I moved here only in April, still it was damn cold, snow everywhere, but I love it. My cat isn't so keen on the cold but he's an indoor kitty, you know? He has to watch out the window from the condo. And you? Are you passing through? What did you say your name was? Will I have read any of your books?"

I sat back and put the notebook on the bar. "No," I laughed. "I doubt it, but here's a card with the website and name in case you want to! Where did you move here from?"

People love questions about themselves. Dave shared his nachos and we settled into sharing some background stories, although mine stayed brief as usual. For all I write, I hate talking about myself. It brings up how different I am, the Ex-pat, the scruffy middle-aged woman with shaggy hair, a van and three pets. I kept bouncing the questions back, Dave didn't notice. He told me of moving from San Francisco, and how he now worked at the condo as the manager and maintenance super. A good job he told me. But when Dave excused himself for a bathroom break, another voice caught my attention. And held it.

"Did you say you're a writer?"

All around families ate out this Sunday, a sunny day outside but with a bite in the air. A reminder of the altitude, the Grand Tetons in the near distance, the cloud cover hid them from me but I knew where to glance. Multiple TVs flickered in my peripheral vision but the man next to me had caught me. An unassuming presence, calm, introverted, confident, with working hands, rough and scarred. His pale blue eyes caught me. I'm not easily caught. I didn't fight it. I listened, genuinely this time. I asked questions, I took notes. Frank laughed and told stories. What was the difference between the two men? Both in their fifties, slightly older than me, one indoor and one outdoor. It wasn't even that though. It was that Frank had moved to Jackson in 1979 with a couple of sled dogs and now he is one of the most well known and respected sled dog breeders and trainers. He'd been a professional dog musher for 23 years and had learned from one of the greats of the Iditarod. He breeds, raises, works the dogs and even takes tourists like myself on tours with the dogs during winter. He was slender, about 5'10" with buzzed grey hair and in his Sunday best clean black jeans and denim shirt.

"I don't raise them to sell them. I train them, each of them; we have about two hundred right now. One by one, they are born at the ranch, they work, and when they're too old to do anything but sleep and eat, there is a retirement community for them. Right now, I have five puppies under three months and ten old-timers. Did you pass through Pinedale? You'd have passed my place. Come by some time if you like, but call first."

I laughed, "probably not a good idea, I have two wimpy dogs and a cat called Stephen in the van with me. They'd have a fit if I brought them to yours."

Frank grinned and bought us both a pint. He made me pull out my pen again.

"So when you leave here, head north okay? You want to go through Lamar Valley, have you heard of it? No? Okay, so head towards Cooke City and Paradise Valley. I want you to check out Chico Hot Springs, great place. You'll not believe it. Well worth a slight detour. You said you're going to Washington, aren't you? Well, that's good. Heading through Montana, stay at the Flathead Reservoir. You'll like it, dark grey and stormy, a huge lake that often you can't see the other side."

"Well, it was nice to meet you Sarah."

Dave stood behind us, nervously offering a handshake. I'd forgotten him, hadn't even noticed his return. I'm sorry Dave but Frank had better stories, what can I say? Dave left with another shy smile and my guilt built and then was forgotten again as Frank gave me his number.

Harold, or Harry as Rosie calls him, came home with

me on my birthday one May. I'd just moved onto my land, twenty acres, a shack, and an adobe garage that would make a great home at some distant point. With a school bus to live in, one that'd been with me for eight years, it was time to get another dog. Daisy had died three years before and having lost my home that same year, I'd not been ready. Maybe it was time? Mark, a friend, worked at the Santa Fe Animal Shelter and called me that week.

"We have a litter of Border Collie mixes. Wasn't Daisy one? Are you interested? They'll go fast though." We chatted briefly, and he told of the litter being found in a box on Airport Road. "All shots and fixed, healthy considering that night outside. They're lucky to be found so quickly."

Later that day I drove to town and yes, checked out the puppies. Seven weeks old, fat, furry black and white with floppy ears, they all bounced around, too many to count, yipping and squealing. I liked them but walked away empty handed. But then I couldn't sleep that night. At nine in the morning when the shelter opened, there I stood with an empty coffee cup in hand, anxious. Mark laughed but reassured me that there were still four of them.

"Come on in. You know where to go."

He followed my long stride to the puppy room, a

sterile twenty by fifteen space with six different kennels
for the various litters. The Border Collies were in the
first kennel on the right. "What's his story?" I pointed
to a shy little fella hiding in the far corner, covered in
puppy poop. He barely made eye contact with humans
or siblings.

"That's Harold. He's terrified by all the noise. A bit
of a nervous Nellie, if you ask me."

"I'll take him."

"Are you sure? He's kind of a wimp, you'll be
protecting him, not the other way round."

"I'll take him."

That was that pretty much that. Mark stepped
among the three others, picked Harold up gently and
passed him over the short brick wall into my arms. The
pup stank, shook, then buried his head in my armpit,
took a deep breath and stopped trembling. It was love. I
took him.

The directions to the free camping in the Gros Ventre
led me into a gated community beside Snake River, one
of mansions and empty homes. I parked anyway and let
the critters explore until tired. Off to find a place to
stay, I simply followed the signs into the National
Forest up towards Slide Lake, yes, so named because
the hill slid into a valley, closing it off to create a lake.

Atherton Campground was twelve dollars, which was the most I'd spent so far but worth it as we found the last site on the lake itself. Firewood was easily scavenged, the dogs ran wild and Rosie swam. Harold paddled. Stevie climbed trees. Just another night camping with the family.

In the morning, we explored early before anyone was up. Harold though, sweet Harold the non-fighter charged up hill and jumped a floppy Golden retriever, not that I could shout, everyone was asleep. The owner ran up to the dogs at the same time as me, after I'd huffed my way up the hill. Luckily the young man was completely unfazed and told me to 'have a nice day, and don't worry, it's a dog thing.' Smiling he leashed his pup and wandered back to his travel trailer.

I muttered to Harold, "We've talked about this!"

Harold hung his tail low and stayed close. "He looked at you funny. I was just doing my job." He sulked.

Rosie of course was oblivious, too busy stalking a squirrel by the camper.

The Grand Tetons, oh my, the Grand Tetons made my week. The description of this NW entrance to the park was of an 'extremely narrow winding road', exciting it sounded so we took Wilson Road to get there, crossing the river once more. The clouds had lifted, the sun shone, and the critters were happily looking out the windows but not trying to escape. What more did I need? Moose road into the National Park was indeed a one-way gravel narrow track but more like a lane in Worcestershire than some off road wild ride. That said, it winds along the base of the Tetons; you glimpse them from below like a toddler looking at his parent, in awe, bending backwards to smile up to the face above. Glorious. I'd also made peace with bears. Here we were in the parks, in the mountains of Wyoming, the signs for bears and wildlife covered all notice boards. Here I would see a bear in a safe and comfortable environment. The rangers were everywhere. What could go wrong? Nothing. I didn't see a single bloody bear.

The Tetons were formed some thirteen million years ago by a fault line, with one block shifting up and the other down. There are no foothills as such; it's a dramatic sudden rise of seven thousand feet from valley to glacial peaks. It was truly stunning, such sharp mountains with a mix of coniferous forests, meadows, and alpine streams.

Jenny Lake was on the tourist trail, the main paved loop in the park itself, but that summer, the roads were closed by construction so we all were confined to a smaller area than normal. Snowmelt and a few glaciers fed Jenny Lake, another dramatic deep dark blue lake that blew me away. The tourist buses, the cars, the bicycles, the mass of people all walking down the path with me didn't take away the beauty and peace from staring at Jenny for an hour. I even stopped worrying about the pets, none allowed on paths in the national parks, only on paved roads and parking lots, poor buggers. But I forgot them, lost in the colors and details of the waterfalls on the far side, the snow melting down the craggy steep mountains, the soft haze of clouds building. Incredible. Stunning. Did I say that already?

"What's that, Hawold?" Stevie peered through the windscreen, his voice small in awe.

Harold shook his head but Rosie offered a timid, "Big?"

Early that morning as we drove back towards town, a herd of bison stopped traffic on Highway 191. Cars pulled over to the edge, families emerged with cameras in hand as these monstrously sized shaggy animals walked amongst the vehicles, comfortable with the attention. I breathed in deeply and explained bison to the critters.

"A long time ago, a bison population of over 20 million dominated the country from the Appalachian mountains to the Gulf coast and Alaska. Since the 1800s they've been killed almost to the point of extinction, counting only a thousand or so in the early 1990s, but now with new regulation, some 50,000 bison live in the states, and perhaps five thousand in Yellowstone and the Grand Tetons. They can run as fast as 30 miles an hour, so don't try anything funny, guys."

Stevie didn't move but for his tail twitching in time to the lecture, and he flinched when one bull headed our direction. Windows closed, dogs froze in place, and the van was silent. The bull wandered across the road without a glance.

"Phew, that was close. Can we go now?" Stevie jumped down and crawled under the bed. "I'm taking a nap. I don't want to see another one of those, okay?"

"Wow, that was cool!" Rosie grinned at me. "Did you get a photo?"

Bridger-Teton National Forest covered the eastern side of the Jackson Hole (what they call the actual valley) with little by way of signs. I'd studied the maps in detail and found Pacific Creek Road, a relatively wide gravel road that led us up and away from the RVs. Quiet. I needed to be alone. The traffic and noise even in a national park like this overwhelmed me, over stimulated even as I craved being around people. Tiring to go back and forth like this, but whatever works, right? A pullout within the lodge pole pines and on the side of a broad meadow was a perfect respite. Teatime, sandwiches, and a walk with all three critters off-leash, and yes, bear-spray in my pocket. No bison here, Stevie was glad to see.

I never did call Frank.

YELLOWSTONE, WYOMING

If you like tall never-ending pine trees lining highways full of RVs, trailers, and vans like mine, you'll love Yellowstone National Park.

I didn't.

HEBGEN LAKE, MONTANA

Now this I liked: A lake, free camping, and trees. Empty. Quiet. A table. Firewood. Campfire. Happy critters. Yep, this I liked. And only half an hour from Yellowstone, more or less en route to Flathead Reservoir in Montana, we'd lucked out again.

"What are we doing?" Harold sat next to me by the campfire, overlooking the lake. We lazily watched the youngsters explore off leash, Stevie up a tree and Rosie in a hole. He leaned in for a scratch. "What are we doing?"

"Camping." I found his tickle spot and his left leg twitched.

"I know that, but why? Aren't you getting lonely?"

I sighed and stopped scratching him, sitting back in the folding chair. "No, I have you to talk to, don't I?"

Harold sighed and stood up, walking away.

I drank a tepid beer, my full belly after a dinner of Frito pie and tortillas. The night was perfect, the forest not too dense, and a lake that spread out of sight east and west. No one came to the campground and a couple in their thirties slowly paddled past in a double kayak, nodding in surprise when Stevie jumped down and ran to the van. I toasted them with an empty beer bottle and hoped they would/ wouldn't stop and talk to me.

So what is it about camping alone that I like so much? The quiet. The lack of words thrown at me to kill an uncomfortable silence. For me though it's not uncomfortable, I like it. Always have, and for most of my life tried to pretend otherwise. It makes others uneasy when they know I like being alone, the pitying expressions of how I'll 'find the right man/ woman some day', followed quickly by the phrase, 'don't give up hope.' Hope? Where do I begin with that? I don't.

Finally I'd found an ease in myself, happiest on my own with the pets by a lake and a campfire. This truly was my happy place. A social introvert. But Harold was right, I guess, there's something odd about talking to him.

Dating at my age is apparently an issue for some friends of mine. They dream of, talk of, and yes, plan for a long-term relationship. The job description is posted on Okcupid or some such website. They interview prospective partners and ask about long-term goals, the reasons other relationships broke up, and the patterns to be worked on. Only then do they set up a date, that is, once the negotiations are complete and a provisional contract agreed upon. And I'm the one pitied? For being single and happy? Aren't they coming at this the wrong way? Anyone will do as long as the right boxes are checked, the agreements made, and contract signed. Really? Yes, really. And I pity them, I do. I know it's politically incorrect to say such a thing but it's true. Don't you want to meet someone you really like, and then realize you want to spend more time with them? In a month, a year, congratulate and celebrate the time spent together?

"It's you I want to be with, to get to know you, whatever that might entail! Damn, I'm excited to find out!"

Versus:

"You have the correct answers, the right sized baggage, okay. We'll plan on a long term relationship, what do you think, married in two years?"

Rosie jumped onto bed, sock in mouth, desperately trying not to lick me. Her tail slapped against Harold and he huffily jumped down. Rosie sat on my chest, wagging, smiling, and singing the song of my mum's morning greetings.

"The sun has got its hat on, hip hip hip hip hooray, the sun has got its hat on and it's coming out to play!" Tuneless but effective, she spat the sock onto the bed.

Stevie joined the chaos, bringing his claws and purring fur onto the pillow. Harold sat by the door, whimpering. That was all it took for me to jump up, quick glance outside and then open the doors wide. The three made a break for the trees.

"Did you smell that bear last night?" Harold finished his breakfast with a sigh and lay down in the sunshine. Rosie licked at his bowl before doing the same. Stevie was a free agent and loving every second.

Bear? Here? Damn it. Well, it made sense, West Yellowstone, a vibrant tourist town, was only ten minutes away, the mountains and national park not much further, where all those thousands of grizzlies lived in safety. Yellowstone has the absolute most grizzlies in the States, a great detail I tried to ignore.

"Stevie! Where are you, kid?"

His little white head popped out from behind the tall grass. "What now?"

"Nothing."

He sank down, ready to stalk another fly.

Bears, damn it. But I liked it at Hebgen Lake, which spreads out over 12,350 acres, wide and deep blue with ducks everywhere. Nearly every night so far we'd stayed by a lake or river. The ocean called though: I craved a wide-open grey afternoon at the ocean. Only a thousand miles or more. What's the big rush? I sat back with the coffee and planned the week ahead, researching rural towns to visit, back roads to follow and lakes to camp beside. Easy enough when you have full size atlases for each state you're passing through. The morning passed lazily.

Why are we here though? It was a valid question of Harold's. To escape a shitty situation? Running away? No, I can't say that's the case. More like I'm running towards something, I just don't know what it is. I really didn't know what I was looking for, only that it was something different. I was bored (am bored) with my life in New Mexico, needing a bigger perspective, a more worldly view hopefully. The usual conversational starts with 'what did you do today?' Then progresses onto how drunk so-and-so was the night before, followed by 'Are those new socks?'

Sheesh. Yes, it was time to hit the road. My goal was to explore a region of the States I didn't yet know, the Northwest. The route, roughly speaking, was to take us up through Colorado, into Wyoming, Montana, Washington, Oregon, and back through Idaho. The coast called. So many random conversations pointed me towards Washington and Oregon that the plan was to spend at least a month along the smaller highways from Bellingham towards Northern California and then head back home. I was on sabbatical, remember? Deadlines and all of that nonsense.

The real question in my mind was where could I move? My next community? My tribe? Where were they? Who are they? Yes, if I were a good girl and got back to TJs in time, I could in theory relocate and transfer with them later on. So that made me plan visits to the smaller cities with TJs, to check out, consider, get a feel for...but did I want to work in a store for much longer? Let alone for the rest of my life? I'd got caught up in the whole regular paycheck, retirement, and those limited conversations based on fear.

Until I met Shaun and Casey: They woke me up,

reminded me of better days, more interesting days, and reminded me how the travelers' life is my natural state. Ah, Shaun and Casey. Shaun is a whole nine months older than me, and I remind him as often as possible. An outdoor dog, a kayaker, sailboat (re)builder, five foot ten, fit, strong, dark hair and goatee, with sparkling eyes buried under the inevitable hat he wears inside and out. He's a storyteller, ongoing, 'did I tell you about?' kind of talker, repetitive and fascinating both. Born and raised in Australia, we bond over the Ex-pat syndrome, or is it status? Laughter, tall tales, and many a beer were enjoyed with Shaun and Casey for the few months before leaving on the trip. Casey though? She's smaller, less pushy socially, yet a talker herself, like when she came over to mine to work out some website ideas, we spent the afternoon chatting and giggling over my computer, planning escapes for all of us.

If anything, my mum would blame these two for getting me back on the road. Bless them. And Mum, Dad, if you were here, I'd bring them both up to Hill Farm House, they'd set up a tent in the field behind home, and make a campfire, cooking you dinner as they kept us all entertained. I wish you could have met each other.

Instead though, the campfire crackled for yet another morning as we devoured our breakfasts, me and the three animals I call my furry family.

The social need came out though, the grocery stock diminished, and it was time to head into West Yellowstone for an afternoon. With a tarp, my chairs, dog bowls, and other odds and ends to claim our spot, I packed up the critters and off we took, a short drive to town to replenish the reserves.

West Yellowstone repels most of my 'traveler' friends; they hate the tourism, the glossy signs, the fake bears and elk on the street corners. Me? I laughed outloud at the bad puns and yes, loved every corny moment, not a snob this time around. There are two main highways through town, Hwy 191 of the last few weeks, and the start of Hwy 20 heading west, the way I'd be leaving when ready. Hwy 20 would take me through Montana and towards the NW Overland Rally in Plain, Washington.

Yep, West Yellowstone, home of cheap groceries and a laundromat. That was all I needed. Well, I'd hoped to find a pub that appealed, but nothing did, so with another six-pack, we headed back to camp.

The place was full. What the hell happened in those three hours? Cars, tents, trucks, and even an old RV claimed all ten campsites. Social hour at Hebgen Lake. I made a fire, let the critters roam before tucking them up inside for bed. Bears, you know, they wander around at night, or so Harold reminded me by sniffing deeply, nervously, before walking slowly back to the van.

Butter, a young corgi, wandered over with a couple in their thirties following, the owners of the classic RV, an old Winnebago. Francesca and George came from Wisconsin, just north of Madison, and so we chatted about some of the places we both knew in town, the Crystal Corner tavern still stands apparently. They'd been on the road for a month or so, heading west they said. AJ, in the tent and bicycle, a scruffy and bearded redhead told us of his travels from Minnesota. His stories ended with "Maybe it's because I'm a dude?"

He showed no interest in our stories, too young to care. He stood with feet wide apart, and I almost pointed out that if he kept his feet together he wouldn't be so short.

Elizabeth and Victoria, both in their early twenties, worked for an oil company in New Jersey and had taken a couple of weeks to drive out west in an old Camry. They set up a tent near me, talking away, sipping on beers, smoking, and then hanging out by my campfire telling me about driving 1,500 miles in only a few days, sleeping in truck stops etc. Both kids were wired and hyper, funny for an hour but then I craved the silence of my van. But listening to them, it reminded me of those long ago days of my twenties, old fart that I am…Well, no, I never did rush it like those two, always took my time on the road, it took me six months to get from New York to LA my first year here. It's probably because I'd not had a proper job as such, just self-employed most of my life, either that or woefully unemployed, and too broke to do more than hitch. Oh those days.

I glanced over to the van, with Rosie watching me out the passenger window, and Harold from the side windows, lying on the bed and warming it for me. Yep, the good life. Then Victoria lit up another joint and started talking about God and that was that. I made my excuses and left them to it. God? Dog? I know which I prefer.

LAKE INEZ, MONTANA

In the middle of bloody nowhere.

It had been a long tiring day, over mountain passes with snow only a few hundred feet from Highway 287 and Quake Lake. Valleys opened up, mountains closed in. The freeways wound into and around rivers, hills, and a few small rural towns that didn't appeal in any way: I didn't stop. Time to move, to shake it up a little. Stevie no longer needed his magic pills although Rosie asked for them; she liked that dopey feeling apparently.

We drove onwards, stopped under a bridge for sandwiches and a pee-break. Stevie, well, I trusted him more, and so he got to walk with the big dogs now, off leash, following along, bouncing to keep up with Harry, and tripping me up if I didn't pay attention. One lake after another, one small town after another, I couldn't stop, don't know why. It was one of those days: Must keep driving. Must keep driving.

"Fuck I'm tired," I muttered as we waited to fill up at a gas station in Clearwater.

"Can't we stop? I'm bored." Rosie whined. "I need to run, I do, and this is cruel and unusual punishment, that's what Harold says."

"Oh is it?"

Harold looked out the window, saying nothing.

"Should I carry on for another hundred miles for Seeley Lake? Or get to Hungry Horse?" I pondered our options, maps, and my energy levels.

"Did you say, hungry?" Stevie popped up onto the dashboard. "I'm hungry!"

All three stared at me hopefully, but then when the engine started, they said nothing but assumed their positions.

"Soon, we'll be there soon," I lied.

Montana was wet. No sunglasses needed. Lake Inez the

sign said, and under it an even smaller sign for a campground. Down a steep hundred-yard track and then north again, I drove slowly, eyeing up a good spot for the night. A deep canyon was filled with this little known lake, which spread north to south, and the campground was more along the line of dispersed sites with fire pits and nothing more. Perfect. Well, good enough. Under a circle of tall pines, we set up camp. Doors opened. Critters explored. Fire made and dinner served. It had been a long day, and yes, Rosie ran herself silly chasing squirrels. We all slept deeply. No signs warning about bears. Just cougars.

FLATHEAD LAKE, MONTANA

"Jesus, are we back in Wales?"

Slapped across the face by a spray of freezing water, I yelled in the wind. Waves crashed against the beach, sailboats bobbing in the marina just half a mile away. I couldn't see the far side as the cloud cover was low and heavy with fog, rain, and yes, wind. The dogs loved it. I loved it. With my hood up, glad for the boots I'd brought along for this summer holiday, we hiked around. The parks along this seaside, well, lakeside were within a wealthy, gated and decidedly unfriendly subdivision, not a welcoming place for strangers with dogs. So we crossed private gardens, slipped on muddy grass, swore at the chain-link fencing, and then waded into the lake itself. It was wonderful; every wet minute made me grin and giggle as another wave threatened us. It really did remind me of the south coast of Wales. Dramatic, dark, and appealing. We hiked back to the van, strategically parked at the Flathead Lake Brewery. A brewery with a view. And it was cocktail hour somewhere in the world.

With dogs and Stevie munching on snacks in the camper, I wandered inside with smartphone, glasses, maps, notebook and pen. Ready for a couple of beers in other words. I stared happily out the huge eight-foot windows onto the damp afternoon below. Perfect.

Flathead Lake Brewery stood high above the lake. The lake itself is some thirty miles long and fifteen miles wide. It's the largest freshwater lake west of the Mississippi. David Thompson, an explorer in the late 1800s, first described it as a 'fine sheet of water.' No wonder I felt as if on the edge of the British Isles, the lake is huge. An extensive glacier moved all the way down to Poison at the southern tip of what is now a dam and hydroelectric power plant before slowly melting and retreating northwards. The Rocky Mountain Trench carved out a straight and steep valley extending far away into Yukon. These days the climate is pretty mild considering how far north Bigfork and Kalispell are. I sat at the bar finished my first pint and considered another. The bartender was a healthy outdoors type, with a short beard and buzzed dark brown hair, wearing the brewery's own tee shirt. He grinned as he waited for me to say, what the hell, why not?

"Where are you heading next?" he asked taking my credit card after pouring a second pint. I'd cut myself off, no more until settled in for the night. Looking at my notes, I talked of the need for a free campground for a few nights before heading to Glacier National Park. "There are quite a few down Hungry Horse, that's the plan. Have you been there?" I showed him on the map.

Mike shook his head. "Not yet, I've only been here since April. Seasonal work. I've been up to the Park though. Are you going to Kintla Lake? It's freakin' amazing there, and people'll not overwhelm you, you see it's down the North Fork Road, a rough gravel narrow road, not one for RVs or trailers. You're in that van, right?"

We both turned and yep, Rosie was watching me from the front seat. I grinned automatically. "Yup. Not four-wheel drive but those tires get us most places. So far so good anyway." I tapped knuckles on the wooden bar.

Mike turned the map to see it better and then with my pen, marked out the best routes through Pinebridge. "Get one of their pies, they're famous for them. The blue cheese one is killer." He grinned and wandered off to pour some beers for a table of suits.

HUNGRY HORSE RESERVOIR, MONTANA

Heading down a little gravel road, NF 895, the rain worried me. The mountains on either side of this narrow hidden lake were snow-capped with low heavy clouds lingering despite the afternoon winds. The dogs stuck their heads out the passenger window, ears flapping gently at ten miles an hour. Stevie hung over his shelf, waiting for the engine to stop. The Hungry Horse Reservoir had caught my attention online; a few photos had popped up on some forum, images of a narrow, deep and lengthy Bruce Ridge. I worried that in snow the road would make us slide down into the steep gorge, and those damn rainclouds darkened as we crept along slowly and carefully. For a while, I doubted my notes and thought we'd missed the campground but no, after twenty-four miles a sign pointed east and downhill. Hail and rain hit hard, briefly, surprisingly, and made me glad for the coveralls hanging up in the back. We'll be fine, right?

There was only one other small RV in the campground and so I claimed the far corner, privacy and all that. It's strange to me how often a campground will be empty but for me, a family would then arrive and set up right next to me. So much for a quiet night: Maybe they think I'd be lonely without them? Is it the pack mentality? Not to worry here though, no one was going to be joining us in this hidden canyon.

Rosie however didn't quite get the idea of privacy and she raced over there to say hello, just as I did as a kid camping in Spain with my family. Mum and Dad would be setting up the tent, getting food ready, and I'd wander off to find new friends. For Rosie, it's more about begging if I'm not mistaken.

The storm hovered over the mountains surrounding us, heavy and dark clouds, rain off and on. I sat on the rocks next to the sandy water's edge, sipping a hot tea and watching Stevie explore.

"What will we do if it snows though?" I spoke outloud.

Harold came over and leaned in. "We'll eat, sleep, walk in the snow. Nothing different really." He's such a sensible boy. "I'm hungry." He smiled at the sandwich in my hand. "Really hungry."

"Fine. But you know I've created a monster?" I

handed over the crust. Rosie suddenly appeared.

"Is someone eating? Without me? That RV is empty, no one came out even though I scratched on the door. No one shouted at me either. I don't think we should bother with them Harry, no food there. I'm hungry."

Shaking my head at the two starving abused dogs, I finished my tea and followed Stevie along the rocks and tree trunks, picking up an armful of kindling and logs for tonight. On the opposite lakeside were no signs of life even though it looked like a road followed the waterline. I saw nothing but thick forests and bald mountains.

"Well, like Harold said, we'll just stay here if it snows. It's not like I can drive us out of here on that road. Okay, Rosie, take this log back to the van. Harold, here's one for you. Stevie?"

He jumped down from a tree behind me. "I'm hungry!"

Snow covered the mountains to the east of us on the Flathead Range, also known as the Great Bear Wilderness. Great. Bloody bears everywhere. I made another fire and hunched next to it, fully warmed by a union suit, jeans, sweatshirts, coveralls, and snow boots, topped off with a woolly hat and scarf: Summer in

Montana. Harold took his morning constitutional and Rosie took Stevie down to the rocks again. All were in sight, happy and free to roam, not that I relaxed, bloody bears everywhere. The coffee helped. The fire flickered, having a hard time as all the wood was damp but hey, with the help of a little lighter fuel, it torched up nicely. I sat back and stared at the van. Time to play, time to adjust a few details, as the van was pretty much as it was when bought. Three chairs, one behind the driver which became a place for Rosie at times but other than that, it didn't help me out much, except Stevie used it to reach the top shelf, his bedroom. I sketched out ideas of how to set up as a camper and less a temporary home. A table or desk would make a huge difference, taking out that extra chair, I'd have room for a 40" table with shelves either built in or stashed underneath. Food, kitchen supplies in the shelves. The cooler would fit under the table, and work as a seat when I'm writing or cooking inside. Yep, the water container and the box of dog kibble could fit under there as well. At that point in the trip, everything got pulled out to cook or feed the pets and myself. It was a pain on a rainy day like this but oh well, little at a time, right?

"Stevie said there's a big bird watching him. He's kinda freaked out. Can you come get him?" Rosie wandered over unconcerned but doing her big sister duties. She looked back to the rocks, "he's hiding. You might want to get him. Oh, did you finish that? I can clean up for you if you like?" She stared at the plate on my lap.

"Fuck. An eagle? Hawk? What is it?" I don't know why I asked; Rosie doesn't notice birds. Harold however, Harold loves to chase birds. Typical boy dog.

"Stevie? Are you okay?"

A little meow squeaked out from under a tree trunk. "Over here, I'm over here. Has it gone?"

"Yep, you're safe. Come on little fella. Come back to the van with me. Are you hungry?"

Stevie's white face peered out and looked around cautiously. Harold came up, strutting slightly. "I took care of it. He won't be back, Stevie. Come on, she'll give us treats I bet. She does when she's worried."

Grabbing the cat, and throwing him over my shoulder, we all scrambled up the hill and settled inside to look up the local birds. Apparently Bald Eagles and Kestrels make their homes in the Flathead Valley. Just another threat on my little cat's life, dammit. It's not easy taking Cat Stephen for a ride.

Fuck it. Time for tea and treats. Inside.

WEST GLACIER, MONTANA

Before heading into the National Park, I stopped for some supplies, drinking water, creamer, snacks, beer and ice. The usual. Just past the main entrance, a gas station offered all that was needed so while gassing up, I stepped inside for a minute. I wish I hadn't.

Time for the bathroom before stocking up, I went down the hallway, past the fliers and posters and a group of teenage girls. I stepped into the women's bathroom. Within a minute, the door opened, followed by tentative giggling and whispering.

"He's in here!" Giggle. Giggle. The door closed and silence as I pissed in anger.

I walked out, grabbed the beer and ice and stood next to these girls in line at the cash desk. They went silent as I stood close, very close, and smiled sweetly at them.

"Nice day, isn't it?" I said, making them acknowledge me, with my soft English accent, and my obvious women's voice. "Are you from around here?"

"Yes," squeaked one brave soul.

"Figures."

GLACIER NATIONAL PARK

"I recommend you stay at Bowman Lake campground. The ranger at Kintla isn't very dog friendly." The grey haired ranger at the gateway took the information off my pass and handed over a map. "It's an incredible lake, truly glacial. Take the right after you pass Pinebridge. Oh, and get one of their pies. The steak pie is to die for!" She grinned, "and bring one back for me!"

Bowman Lake is another glacial lake, this one a fraction of what it was even fifty years ago. Glacier NP came into existence during 1910, and within twenty years was joined with the Waterton Lakes National Park of Canada, to create the first International Peace Park of 1,800 square miles, full with over 720 lakes, bighorn sheep, mountains, moose, grizzlies (of course), elk, eagles (sigh) and yes glaciers. Of the estimated 150 glaciers that existed in the park during its early years, only twenty-five remain. Scientists expect that those too will melt by 2030. Sad.

The road was indeed a winding narrow gravel route into the western side of the park, little utilized except by the hikers and campers. With no wide turnouts and too many switchbacks, the road limited the kind of visitors who came this far up the North Fork Road, of which the

"Inside North Fork" road had washed away earlier in the year. The "Outside" road had been maintained and was a pleasant drive through such tall trees as to see none of the mountains on either side of us. The track climbed higher, the road narrowed, and after six miles a campground sign popped up. I took a deep breath in relief.

The campground was run by the Park and as such all critters had to be leashed.

"What? Again? But I hate this rope!" Stevie threw a fit. The pups just hung out, knowing I'd take them for a walk soon enough. Stevie, poor bugger, was pissed at me. Again.

"I'll be good! Honest! I won't go too far, honest, oh come on, please, take this damn thing off me!" He sulked under the van until four horses trotted past. Funnily enough, the van suddenly seemed like a great place to be. I shut the door pretty sharpish and took the dogs to the lake.

Stunning. It was a crystal cobalt blue, untouched and mirror like, and with ragged mountains all around us that had layers of grey white snow in the crevices, glacial creeks dripping down the steep edges like icing on a Christmas cake. A lone kayaker paddled in the distance and the paddles slapped softly. No one was around. I let the dogs off leash, nervously watching for the ranger. Harold and Rosie ran, splashed, but got spooked and sat at my feet, each facing in opposite directions. The colors, the sky, the silence, I couldn't get enough. I took the dogs back to the van and grabbed a beer and camera. We spent the rest of the afternoon staring at the unbelievably beautiful and little used Bowman Lake. It measures seven miles in length and Rainbow Peak climbs to 9,861 feet in the aptly named Cerulean Ridge to the east.

On the walk through the campground, I stopped at the notice board. Wish I hadn't, all sense of relaxation fell fast.

A warning sign: Keep all pets leashed and in sight. Cougar activity in the area has taken dogs from their leashes when left alone. This is serious. Do not leave your pets alone.

"We're leaving tomorrow, kids."

The dogs looked up at me, not quite sure who to blame for my crankiness. Harold, the brave, spoke up first.

"Was it Stevie? I'll talk to him…"

"No, it's not, but thanks kiddo. It's just not safe here for us. And I can't let you run around again, okay? I don't want to lose anyone."

Rosie sniffed my hand. "I'll behave, I'll stay close, honest." She nudged me again.

"Okay, okay, I believe you, but later, okay? We'll walk later."

Back at the van, I unleashed the pups before opening the van door; it's easier that way. Rosie ran into the trees. "SQUIRREL!"

Harold made to chase but with a quick grab of his collar, he was stuck with me. I ran after the mischief-maker and found her with a dead squirrel in the middle of the path. Throwing her in the van with the others, I went back to take care of the corpse when the Ranger wandered up, checking on his campers. We chatted...he didn't mention the dead animal a few feet away. I didn't mention my dogs. We got along just fine.

As my campfire died down, two elk suddenly crashed through the trees. They stopped at my picnic table, all furry antlers and gangly legs, and big. Bigger than I'd imagined, they stood there, looking at the remains of my dinner and then at me, only three feet away. Time stopped and I stared unmoving. A dog barked from inside the van, they flinched and then ran to the next tent.

LIBBY, MONTANA

I missed it. I did. I took the wrong turn, the wrong national forest road, and after going back and forth in the Kootenai National Forest, my sense of direction took a backseat. I stopped on a dirt road next to a river and a railway track. Next to the remains of someone else's fire pit, I set up camp, checking around first before opening the doors. Out they came, Stevie first. At least he said a quick 'thanks' before following Rosie to the river where they both drank deeply.

I don't know how but we'd left at 10 a.m. and took us till 4 p.m. to settle, having covered a mere 160 miles. I'd wanted to explore Montana it's true, had done tons of research into all the lakes and small towns to visit, but so far, I'd raced up to Glacier, driven back through Pinelodge the next day, stopping for a veggie pie and coffee in the morning and now we were in the middle of nowhere, and I didn't have a clue as to how we'd find our way out again. The rain came. A hawk hung out on the towering pines at the edge of the clearing, and I was worn out.

Filling the bucket with river water in the morning, I set about heating enough to wash my short scruffy hair, and to have a thorough sponge bath. Just as I'd stripped off, head in bucket, a train slowly passed, hooting merrily.

WORKING ON THE ROAD

If you thought my days were filled with roads, naps, and beers, you're only getting half of the story. I also had to send in three articles a week for an online magazine, all on dog-related subjects. I'd write up a rough outline, often about my experiences of camping with dogs in all of these places, then find a library to do some final research, add the five photographs, and send it all in once a week. For my websites and blog, I'd work out a basic trip report, pick a handful of photos and schedule postings while on the road. It took a full day at town to catch up on the outside world. It kept me in touch with friends, and with those following along, some interested in the Dirt Roads And Dogs stories and others were fans of Stevie's Big Adventures.

Okay, you're right, it wasn't so bad, only once a week but when it was time to find a library, be in town, do laundry, grocery shopping, it seemed such a chore! I'd make sure all three critters had a big hike in the morning, then we'd head into town before the midday sun hit hard. I had to plan thoroughly, which town to aim for, what supplies were needed, and try to get it all done in one stop. Usually it worked and then we'd retire to more National Forest campgrounds for a few days to recover. So much for talking to locals, much of the time I kept my head down, hid my accent, and got out of there pretty fast.

LIBBY, MONTANA

I missed it again. With a fresh outlook after my bathing by the river, I'd checked the maps and set off for Libby once more. What should have been 30 minutes took an hour and a half. East became west became north. I was so bloody turned around, the sun was hidden by low clouds and tall mountain peaks. The forest service road climbed up a steep dirt track, the right side became a rocky slide down into the valley river far underneath, all clinging to the mountain. Glad I hadn't met another vehicle, when we finally hit paved road, my hands shook.

CLARK FORK, IDAHO

Will, the bartender, told me to bring my dogs out to the tables in front, "everyone's friendly here, don't worry."

He passed a Heineken out the window to me, and a treat for each of the pups. Within minutes Will joined me. He was a tall rangy man in blue coveralls and with long grey beard and rabbit ears. He lit up a pipe, got me to unleash the dogs to wander free for a while. The tavern was a small temporary building he told me, as the original place had burnt down in February and they were raising the money to build another.

"Community, we all pulled together, it's not my place see; I just work here every Tuesday."

"It's Tuesday?"

He grinned and told me how they're getting the funds together. "We have lawn mower races. Everyone finds a motorized machine, older the better, and then we take them to Tom and Mary's place out of town and race them, taking bets, it's the best time of the month that's for sure!" A bark of a laugh got him coughing until another pick-up pulled in. "Talk of the devil, hey Tom! Are you ready for Sunday?"

Tom was a short stocky man in denim and big black boots, he strode up, thrust out his hand to shake mine, and ordered a whiskey straight. He sat at the picnic table opposite me, distractedly petting Rosie who'd nudged him. "You smell my girl, eh? Sorry, no treats in here, good dog eh?"

The whiskey arrived, more locals arrived, some

chatted to me, some carried on as if I'd always lived in that little town of a few hundred. Clark Fork lay at the north end of Lake Pend Oreille in the Idaho panhandle. Yep, another lake, I'm drawn to them, what can I say? And yes, it's also deliberate that I'd check out these little towns with unusual reputations for being home to outsiders. Clark Fork lies on Highway 200 on the roundabout way to Coeur d'Alene, somewhere on my list of places to check out. I really did need to find a place as a new home base: I was suffocating in Santa Fe, unchallenged, disengaged, and bored. It's not that this was running away, but towards a new life, full of community, challenges, and hopefully as a step ahead of an inevitable wildfire and burning bridges.

After leaving the gang at the pub, being told to come back sometime, I'd taken my maps and found a forest service road heading to the southern tip of this reservoir, all dirt, with a campground far away. It sounded perfect. It wasn't.

I shat myself. No, not really, not this time, that was elsewhere, but almost. The reservoir is dug deep into the craggy mountains with no soft curve of a lakeside road; this was a single track climbing switchbacks for twenty miles. The forests were thick with ponderosa pines, cedar, poplar, aspen and birch trees. I couldn't see a damn thing. I finally stopped when possible, took the critters for a walk in the forest then back to the van for sandwiches and tea. Treats for them, Stevie was doing great, coming on walks with us, sticking close, and meowing when we'd gone too far from home. We'd all turn back and escort him to the camper as a family. It was quite adorable really.

Then the rain came. The road became slick and I drove slowly, nervously traveling back to Clark Fork, then took the long way to Coeur d'Alene, no longer knowing where we'd stay the night. Stressed. Thoroughly. The rain passed and the lake tamed my crappy mood, following us down through Sagle and beyond. Beautiful. It is another of the largest freshwater lakes in the Northwest, created by a glacier moving slowly down and then back to Canada, and now reaches forty-six miles in length. It had been a training ground for the US Navy but after Pearl Harbor, the station moved elsewhere. The shoreline is mostly unpopulated, but was there anywhere I could camp? Not that I could find that night.

GARFIELD, IDAHO

"Where the fuck is Stevie? Oh god, not now, not now. I can't take it. STEVIE! Stevie? Please Stevie, please, where are you kiddo?"

We hiked through a deserted hillside campground. The forest closed in on me, the dark was falling fast as were the temperatures. I'd set up camp, let the kids out, and when I'd gone to do the campground paperwork, had tied all three to their harnesses. "I'll just be a minute."

Now though, Stevie's harness lay on the dirt. I cried. I couldn't deal. I couldn't deal. My boy. My little boy. I walked and walked, crying out his name. The dogs ran beside me, up and down through the trees. We walked for ages, all around, calling his name, banging his food dish. Nothing. I headed back to camp and made the fire before dark. I tried again, opening a can of wet cat food.

"I'm hungry!" He popped out from behind a birch tree and wandered over, jumped inside the van and ate his dinner. His white fur was a little dirty with leaves and mud, but otherwise all intact.

I closed the door, drank a beer, and cried.

COEUR D'ALENE, IDAHO

Breakfast, I needed a decent breakfast, a big mug of coffee and time away from the animals. Downtown Coeur d'Alene was a surprise that delighted me. A huge open parking lot was on the edge of the lake of the same name, a gloriously crisp blue, with sailboats, grassy beaches, picnic tables and all within a block of the historic area which itself was beautiful. The buildings dated back to General Sherman setting up fort on the lake in the 1870s after the British ceded the land below the 49th parallel. Of course, Native Americans had owned the land until explorers such as David Thompson came across the territory. These days the Native Americans count for less than 1% of the population.

The downtown area was full of cafes, restaurants, and stores for the tourists and students. Outdoor seating faced the empty roads leading back to the marina and beaches. I'd have liked to stay in the area but suddenly my deadline for reaching Plain, Washington, was approaching faster than I'd wanted. A week to travel across Washington then, starting in Spokane, only 30 miles west of town. First though, a walk around with pups on leashes and Stevie doped up with his magic pills.

SPOKANE, WASHINGTON

Peanut butter.

Bread.

Fruit.

Salad fixings.

Dog food.

Toilet paper.

The list grew as I sat in the van outside of Trader Joes, the first I'd come across on the trip so far. Remember how I'd talked of looking to relocate, well, part of me, the lazy part of me, thought that transferring with TJs would make life easier. An income in a new place would be nice, right?

I walked inside and it was just like Santa Fe, the same bustle, fake smiles, genuine smiles, and business as usual. Eighties music filled the background and quickly my shopping cart was full of goodies, not all on my list. I should know better but at least I'd eaten first, right? At the cashiers, I introduced myself as a fellow crewmember and she rang for her manager.

"A visiting crew member!"

"Is that right? Where are you visiting from?" The mate was tall, white, and bald, just like the managers at home. I had to grin.

"Santa Fe, with Captain Keith. Do you know him?"

Glenn shook my hand, telling me to say hello to Keith when I got back; they knew each other from another store in California. The cashier then chatted away; she'd gotten married in Santa Fe only three years before. I told her of my idea to move.

"This is a great place. Busy at work and Spokane feels like a big city, you know? Lots to do but with all these lakes and wilderness around, we hike all the time. Love it here. I'll tell Glenn about you moving here. I figure it's always good to put a name with a face, isn't it?"

She was slightly shorter than me, and about the same age and build, in her pink TJs shirt and jeans. I did like it there. Gold star for Hillary.

COFFEE POT LAKE, WASHINGTON

How could I resist such a name? Plus it was a free BLM campground in the middle of nowhere with a lake. Perfect after a day in the cities and a crappy night before that. I got a little lost, excited I guess, and had taken a right and not a left. But back on track after a careful five-point turn on a dirt road, I was glad to see a distant and small pond amongst the rolling wheat fields. Thirteen miles later we came upon it. Sheesh.

Down the gravel track and into a campground that stood empty but for one pear-shaped man in a tent, I parked at the other end of the little row of campsites, deep within the cottonwood trees giving me full shade, a picnic table and a fire pit. The lake was only four or five hundred yards across the parking area, mostly used by local fishermen by the looks of it. This was way off the beaten track. Perfect! No animals, no threat of bears or cougars on signs, no other pets nearby, the doors were opened.

"Release the hounds!" I cried out loud in relief.

"I'm a tiger." Stevie followed Rosie on a tour of the campground, tail held high as he pounced on flies and ants. "Gotcha!"

Coffee Pot Lake got its name from who knows where? I couldn't find out. It is famous however for great fishing with crappie, largemouth bass, rainbow trout, and yellow perch. Since I've never fished, I didn't care about that. Instead, with Stevie back in the van after a few hours exploring and climbing trees, I took the dogs around the lake a ways. A hawk's nest clung to a derelict telephone post and the birds dived at me in anger. I shuffled past determined to find a swimming hole. Over the ridge, a beach of gravel and sand faced north, no boats or hikers in sight, just a pissed off bird or two, so I stripped off and swam; it was absolutely glorious. The dogs sniffed out and about, Rosie even swam with me a little while Harold worried about us from the beach, his ears down, muttering to himself about alligators.

That night, I stayed up later than normal, refreshed and so relaxed with Rosie and Harold happily begging from the other camper, and Stevie climbing up and down the tree next to me. What could be better than this? I picked up pen and paper and played with ideas as to how we could live like this full-time. Would we want to though? Some days were so hard on me, on all of us really. Then we had days like this, easy conversations with strangers, great walks in historic towns, swimming in lakes, campfires and stress-free for each of us. Why not keep going? Up and down, it was still better than the deadly routine of Trader Joes, and then a hermitlike recovery from work for my days off, and then back to work once more. I couldn't keep it up for much longer. I'd changed and not for the better. Ideas for income followed along the lines of passive income from renting out my home in New Mexico, renting out the school bus again. It's a converted 1948 26 footer with bed, kitchen, woodstove and a platform, but no running engine or tranny. It's home to guests and travelers alike. I just needed to fix it up again for renting. What else could I do for income? Put my vehicles into the database for the movies filmed in the areas. I have a few, I'd always have something to drive is the theory. Although one day I was heading to TJs when the 4Runner had a flat tire. The motorcycle leaked gas out the carb. Then a couple of miles on the way, the radiator in the 1972 Land Rover blew a leak. No work for me that day. Did they believe me when I called in though? Nope.

Writing obviously is where I want an income to come from. These articles I'd send off each week were on on pay-per-view basis. Better than nothing and it helped get my name out and build experience in producing regularly. The blog was another good practice for writing regularly and since both used photos of mine, I'd been getting back into photography after years away. How though to find more magazines who'd take my work? How to build a freelance career as a travel writer and essayist? The novels I love, but they're bringing in so little, I need to find other sources of income. However, it could just be a case of marketing as they'd won a few awards already. A focus on selling them would help, right? Still, I'd made a list of ideas, suggestions to follow up on later in the week. A to-do list of sorts. That helped.

The idyllic vacation at Coffee Pot Lake was ruined the next afternoon. The tenter, Albert, had his sister and a daughter arrive, nice enough, we chatted and kept to ourselves, congratulating each other on the great view of this small lake, the peace and quiet, "because you never knew it was here! What a lovely hidden treat!"

If only…

A huge modern RV pulled up with a boat on a trailer behind. It set up camp in the middle of the open area, the parking area for day-use, the area between the campsites and the lake. What a lovely view of the RV. I seethed and drank a beer; it was after five by then. The dogs and cat lazily watched the goings-on. The couple waddled about, tying up a lapdog to a tree, trying uselessly to level out the RV with blocks, back and forward they went. Finally satisfied, they started up the generator.

Great. Just great.

Dark dramatic skies built up around us and I retreated to bed, hugging the not-so-feral-anymore cat and reading another book. The rain began and slammed against the roof, sending Stevie under the bed.

The generator ran all night long. Seriously all night long. Humming, knocking, edging into tense dreams.

In the morning, I went over.

Inside the voices bickered, loud and opinionated. Oh great. Here goes. "Excuse me?"

A big gray-haired obese man waddles down the steps to me, wheezing into the oxygen machine strapped to this bulbous waist. "What do you want?"

"I wanted to let you know that your generator kept us all awake last night. Couldn't you have camped away from the rest of us or even just warned us? Albert and his family are in tents."

"So? I got the quietest generator I could. I got rights, you know! I GOT RIGHTS!"

"But no sense of consideration apparently."

"I GOT RIGHTS!" he yelled after me, coughing and wheezing in anger.

Harold watched from the door, "Shall I get him? I could, you know. Me and Rosie, we could get him for you."

Stevie piped up, "Me too! I'm a tiger! I'm a tiger!" Meow. Meow…

NORTHWEST OVERLAND RALLY, PLAIN, WASHINGTON

Early in the morning, I checked the campground, no one was around, and so released the hounds, oh, and the cat. Stevie was tethered, we'd had a talk about it but Stevie was not happy with me. He ran for the trees and I followed, trying to keep up. The dogs ran into the woods too, sniffed, made the most of the trees to pee on, and the dirt to dig in. Stevie aimed for the tallest tree but was thwarted by the damn rope once again. He hated me. I can't say I liked him at that point either.

Still, I'd made him come with us. As we were walking back, a woman cleaning the porta-loos stopped me.

"Did you know that your pets need to be leashed? It's quiet right now, but you really should tie up the dogs."

I nodded sheepishly and called the pups over. "Yes, Marianne, I will."

She blinked at me in surprise, smiled and went to clean the second portable. You see, this was one of the organizers of this gathering. I'd been asked to talk about traveling with pets, and I recognized her but she didn't know me. Almost busted but not quite!

Yep, we'd set up camp within this rally of around a thousand other travelers and four-wheelers, yep, it was mostly four-wheelers, Land Rovers, Jeeps, trailers, roof top tents, and then there was my van, my uncool conversion van that had traveled for a month along the Rockies, all on back roads, with two dogs and a cat. I was pretty proud of us to be honest. Uncool Vans Unite! All one of us...oh, okay, well...Anyway, the rally was set in a couple of huge meadows within walking distance of Plain, a non-entity of a town, more of a store, a diner, and a gas station. I'd hoped for a café, pub, or some kind of hang out joint, a place to sit on a deck and chat to those traveling like me. Instead, each afternoon I'd simply grab a bag of ice, six-pack, and head back to camp. The level of activity overwhelmed me after a month alone. The dogs lay under the van on long ropes, and Stevie was on lockdown. Yes, in the hills and forests I almost trusted him, but here with so many people, vehicles, and other dogs wandering around? Not at all, I was terrified that he'd panic and run. My nights were full of nightmares. My days were full of conversations.

I don't know why, but I've not been able to describe my time here on any forum, blog, or letter to friends. Words fail me. I had fun. I talked and met a ton of interesting folks. I just wanted to get back on the road.

That's what we did. After I'd given my talks about traveling solo as a woman, and another presentation on traveling with dogs, I packed up and left. I didn't go far. Five miles at most. A national forest road on the right lead us off into tall pines and scrubby shrubs, it was a dirt track with little by way of wear and tear. Perfect. I drove a mile and pulled off where another had obviously set up camp recently, as there was a fire pit, an area of flattened grass, and a level spot to call home. Doors open. Dogs free. Cat up a tree. I called Alexis, my closest friend in Santa Fe, and we caught up, a long meandering conversation that grounded me, made me laugh outloud, and not even stress when all three critters disappeared from view. Drinking coffee in the woods that morning showed me exactly how much of an introvert I have become. I wanted to be alone. Yet there I was chatting to a friend and enjoying it. Virtual friendship better than physical presence? Sometimes, not so much with those like Alexis, but the connections made over the weekend wore me out. I forget I sound different, a mildly English accent affected by an adulthood spent in New Mexico, the tattoos on my knuckles, the scruffy tomboy appearance, and yes, my uncool van were all up for comment. I don't want to be seen as different. I'm not trying to be anything but myself. Leave me alone!

I was alone. Where the hell are my animals? "Anyone hungry?"

Rosie ran up, nose full of fresh dirt, a wide smile, and wagging tail. "Always!"

"Where are the boys?" I asked out of habit.

Rosie looked behind the closest bunch of shrubs, "back there, not far. Don't worry, you can feed me first. I won't tell."

I wandered around the hedgerow and found Harold deep within a newly dug hole and Stevie on a tree trunk next to him, supervising loudly. A raven flew over, squawked once, and Stevie ran for cover. Harold dug away happily, coming up for air. "Oh hello! There's something down here, I don't know what, but I'll share it with you. Hey ho, it's off to work we go!"

TWISP, WASHINGTON

I can't say this town name without a lisp, sorry, it's just the way it is. We'd backtracked to head north into another area of forests and lakes, my comfort zone. The supermarket took me by surprise, as it was stocked full of amazing European cheeses, racks of quality wines, organic produce and healthy groceries. Here? In the middle of the mountains? Why? I asked around. Apparently Twisp With A Lisp is a destination town for those from Seattle and Spokane, amongst other big cities. Full of campgrounds, lodges, bed and breakfasts, this little town in the middle of the Methow Valley has a small permanent population of under a thousand but many more arrive in the summer and fall seasons. The town was first developed by white explorers in the late 1800s, displacing the local Methow Indians as usual, whose population went from 1,200 to 300 within only a few decades, smallpox being a huge cause of so many deaths. The explorers had found gold of course, mining boomed as not just gold, but silver and copper were found in the area. Then timber and agriculture became the main incomes until more recently tourism took a hold with the new highway through the Cascades, opening up the valley to full time retirees, recreation seekers, and all the new businesses needed to serve their needs.

From one culture to another is the story of the Methow Valley and the Native Americans who'd lived there for thousands of years. The same old story wherever exploration and mining happened in the 1800s. Sad.

The directions were fairly clear, but I still got lost up Lightning Creek Ridge. Upper Beaver Creek Road hid behind a sign for a local lake, not one I'd noted on my map, so I missed the turn-off and had to back track. Both reversing and making three or five point turns were becoming easier as time passed. Left on Blaky Hill. Right at the T-junction. Left over the bridge and north into the foothills of the Cascades. Incredible, beautiful and as usual we drove on a narrow steep-sided canyon dirt track. At the peak, I pulled off next to the only tree up there and settled in on a relatively level spot for the night. Doors open. Dogs run free. Stevie climbs the lone tree.

It truly was incredible. Hot, mind you, but it was truly breathtaking. Across the track to the northwest stood the bald and snowy peaks of the Cascade

Mountains, our next destination. The meadows were a burst of wildflowers, with a mix of cowslip, daisies, sunflowers, grasses and purple tiny blossoms unfamiliar to me. The sky was dark blue with only a handful of fluffy white innocent clouds, no threat of rain or snow. These foothills were gently rolling with only a few small woods as there had been a huge wildfire some years before, taking out most of the wildlife and forests. What remained though was phenomenally lush and quite striking as we walked up the dirt road further, all four of us. Stevie was panting hard at the altitude. I picked him and threw him across my shoulder and he actually purred. My feisty little feral tiger purred. He sure has come along way on this trip. Before we left it was rare that he would let me stroke him more than once, twice, three times, and stop! Or be scratched. Nowadays, this little fella would curl up next to my back and purr himself to sleep, even after days on lockdown. On walks, there he was, trying to keep up with his best friend Rosie, running ahead, and stopping to get his wind back. He'd hide behind a blade of grass until Harold ran past, and jump out, making Harry squeak each time. The sun beat down on us and after stretching our legs enough, I carried the tiger back to the van and a stream that appeared out of the rocks behind us.

Perfection. Just what we all needed. Open rangeland for me to have a clear view of any threats to my little furry family. A water source for washing and cooling off in. Hikes. Mountain views. A campfire. Good food. And an okay book. I must remember to get better books when in the next town. Anything.

Suddenly four Jeeps drove past, fully loaded with spare gas tanks, roof top tents and shovels strapped to muddy machines. The drivers stared at us in amazement, at our little 2wd camper van and of course at Stevie who stared back.

The next day we drove back down and through Twisp With The Lisp and into Winthrop. A bookstore on the left, traffic on the right, I kept going, don't know why, but we were in a rush to get into the Cascades National Park. I did need a book still.

BELLINGHAM, WASHINGTON

The list. The plan.
Trader Joe's for dog food and treats, plus to check it out as a possibility for a transferring here.

Chuckanut Brewery (just because).

Hwy 11 along the coast (recommended by James).

Lummi Island, Sammi Island and Pigeon.

Find Internet and upload a few videos and articles.

Laundry.

Bookstore, I was desperate.

Pet store, more calming treats for critters.

"But it's an emergency!"

My voice squeaked in mid panic mode. Traffic flew past, honking horns at my imperfect parking job. The city mayhem overwhelmed me. The critters lay quietly on their beds, shocked at the level of activity and noise outside.

"It's a grinding, metallic, I'm-falling-off sound. Please help me!" I gave her the full story, describing the pets, van, travels, but no, she didn't budge.

"Thursday at nine. I can put you in for Thursday at nine."

"But today's Friday!"

"We're a busy shop, miss. I can't help you before Thursday."

I hung up. Fuck her and her schedule. I wanted to scream, yell, beat the shit of some metal contraption that was not my beloved Van Dreamy. The Van Nightmare of scary noises, scraping metal, knocking bearings, dying axles, and no one could help me. I started up the engine, pulled back on to one stupidly busy main road and drove slowly, nervously, eyeing up signs for mechanics. I found one just off Alabama Street at Woburn, and pulled in. Close to tears, I explained to the young fella who wiped his hands on his overalls before telling me to drive inside. He'd take a look.

The boss was out on an errand; the two lads had almost finished the jobs on hand, and were keen to help. This side road was so quiet in comparison to the rest of Bellingham, that is the little that I saw between Hwy 11 and Trader Joes; it was a mix of small trade shops and tidy homes. With the cat in his big crate, tied to a rope as well, and all windows closed to within an inch, I left the camper with Tom and Johnny, the two mechanics both in their mid-twenties, energetic and enjoying the challenge of diagnosing the issue. I walked the dogs, slowly, breathing in the small town feel of this neighborhood. I could live here, I thought. I might have to stay here, I reminded myself. The dogs peed and pooped. The quiet streets calmed me. I walked and walked; the pups loved it, keeping their questions to themselves, although there were murmurings from Rosie, quickly hushed by sensitive Harold. They were on best behavior.

"We can't find anything, miss. We even took it around the block, making turns, back and forth, doing everything we could. I took the wheels off, there is some play with the front bearings, but it can't be that.

I'm sorry."

Not sure whether to be happy that nothing was wrong, or worried because it wasn't my imagination, I thanked Tom and even though he didn't want to charge me, I gave them each $20 cash as a thanks for going out of their way. Grins and offers to help if I needed to come back, "just ask to speak to us in person, okay?"

I headed off to Fairhaven, some called it South Bellingham, but the locals liked to be a separate entity. It had a completely different feel anyhow; it was slow moving, on the coast with a port and small marina, a local park along the water's edge, a plaza with a bookstore, café, Internet, murals, and even a pet-store. With Stevie still on lockdown, poor bugger, we wandered around. I could live here, I thought, briefly. I might have to.

Jolene had recently moved to town from Tulsa, Oklahoma, and she was ecstatic in her enthusiasm. I can't blame her, what a shift eh? Jolene handed out treats to the pups and we explored the fancy pet store where she worked. So many kinds of bones and treats, the dogs couldn't believe their luck. Rosie found a shelf with rawhide, just the right height for her nose and she grabbed one, bringing it to me and putting it in my hand. "Can I, please? Pretty please?"

"Sure, you've been very patient, kiddo. Harry, want

to find something?"

As I paid up, Jolene told me of the park, and the new pathway that follows the coastline for a few miles, great for the dogs, families, yep, if we had time to go there. "It's beautiful, especially on a sunny day like this."

She handed me some change and put the rawhide into a paper bag. "Just walk down hill and turn right, it'll be about a ten minute walk."

We drove there.

ANACORTES, WASHINGTON

"Can I stay here? Please? My van is dying; I daren't drive it anymore. And it's the weekend, no-one wants to see us until Monday!"

The security guard put away his notebook and smiled, "sure, miss, let's park you over there on the grass though. That's a better spot for you, just keep the dogs leashed, and go tell them at the marina, and I'll check on you later. We have 24 hour security, so you don't need to worry about a thing."

Glorious, it was absolutely glorious. Despite my stress over the noises from the front wheel, the sight of all those sailboats lifted my spirits beyond measure. The sky was crisp cobalt, with lapping waves against the marina as a soothing soundtrack. There was even a grassy field only a couple hundred yards away from shore that was to be home for a couple of days. I let the dogs out, off leash, and they explored a tad before coming back to us, it was dinnertime after all. Stevie, well, Washington was not a good place for my little tiger. He knew it, he hated it, but he no longer attacked my hands out of frustration. I was okay with that, progress of sorts.

Cap Sante Marina welcomed us into their sailing world, offering laundry, a café, showers, books, and all within a ten-minute walk to old town Anacortes on Fidalgo Island. Leaving Bellingham, I'd relaxed for the first twenty miles but then the crunching began again, and I'd pulled off onto Highway 20 West. Finding a small side road, I'd stopped, parked, reversed, pulled forward, backed up again, and driven off soundlessly. Whatever works, right?

Cap Sante Marina caught my attention with all the masts tinkling in the afternoon sun. Glistening clean, obviously expensive, and huge white sailboats lined up against the town's northern edge. A sight for sore eyes, I'd not been able to relax in Bellingham, and that was depressing, as it really had been one of my chosen destinations. Bellingham was a city that had appealed, with my happy memories of Jacob and Billy picking me up from the Ketchikan ferry one summer's day. Trader Joes was there as a potential job, it was a college town, on the ocean, with islands and mountains all within easy reach. It sounded perfect in theory. Yeah, I'd loved the sound of it, the idea of it, but the reality of crazy busy streets, built up corridors of business and warehouses, homes and condos, I hated it. Perhaps though it was because of Van Dreamy acting up? Perhaps. It doesn't matter. I didn't like it.

In Anacortes I relaxed and read about the area. For more than 10,000 years the Samish and Swinomish Tribes lived hereabouts, and yes when the European explorers, trappers, loggers and settlers came, the Native Americans were pushed out, their populations reduced through sickness and conflicts, and now there is only a very small reservation on the southeastern corner of the Island. Same old story wherever I find myself. Sad. Wrong.

These days, Anacortes is a place for the wealthy and those who work the businesses needed by those retirees, sailors, oil refineries, and artists. It's quite a mix as you wander the streets and marina. Everyone I met was incredibly friendly, offering stories, advice, recommendations, but my brain was so fried by worrying about the van and the pets that I remember little but the sight of the masts in the darkening mists. Glorious. Shining white hulls, red trim, flagpoles and masts by the hundreds, I read that there were 940 slips, and in July, all were taken. I sat outside the van that first evening and finished my dinner of lentil stew and tortillas. The sun was setting behind me, and it flickered on the highest of flagpoles, glittering as the night came down. I drank a beer and relaxed as the dogs chewed on rawhide and Stevie stared at me through the window saying nothing nice.

We stayed a few days, taking it slow in the mornings, even letting a tiger roam free for an hour or so, closely supervised by myself and Harold. I'd not feed Stevie until after an hour outside. The refrain 'Anyone hungry?' worked a treat at nine in the morning.

Wandering around the town on foot, I stocked up on people watching but not conversations. I needed silence. On the edge of one small grassy park a sign stood propped over a bowl of water: Dogs Only. No Cats Allowed. Rosie had a good giggle about that.

Walking through another park, the track suddenly opened up to a small sandy beach facing the bay. An old notice was leaning against a rock, the words barely legible: Vessel Not Abandoned. Official or concerned can contact us. Stay clear please. We plan to float out of here this sunset. 3/7/16.

They'd made it out evidently.

We found also some working docks, the port for oil tankers on Shannon Point and even stared at warehouses full of ships being repaired, held high off the concrete floors and surrounded by huge machinery. One afternoon we drove down Burrows Bay and came across a small beach next to a Deception Pass State Park. The campground was full, deep within tall trees but close to the ocean, tempting me to check it out but far too busy for my furry family. We stopped at Biz Point instead, a day-use area full of families and dogs and kids running and screaming, not normally something I can deal with, but that afternoon, watching the sun setting amongst all these people was wonderful. The dogs and I lay on the grassy bank and all three of us napped, dozing to the shrieks of the kids playing in the sand.

"I could live here. Well, we might have to," I reminded myself, sitting up, suddenly stressed about the van again. "Great. Okay, okay, I'll find a mechanic on Monday."

"I don't mind staying here," offered Harold, leaning in for another head scratch.

Rosie's ears turned to us. "Not bad, not bad at all." She fell back asleep with a blade of grass sticking out of her mouth as her tail wagged against my leg.

WARM BEACH, WASHINGTON

Along the Puget Sound, rolling green agricultural fields contrasted nicely to the mountains, wilderness, and the Cascades, which were all tall, dramatic, with tons of small forest roads that appealed but I never got to explore except on my maps. I was on a deadline. Dawn. I had to meet Dawn. I had to find Claire and family. All in the same few days. Why? Well, Claire was heading to Kentucky with the girls on the weekend. Dawn, a friend from my first days in the States, she also had limited time to come from Seattle to see me because of work schedules. I'd been able to arrange meeting them together the same week.

I drove down various small highways, avoiding the I5 completely, although we did pass under it twice in Mount Vernon. South of that little old town, I stopped suddenly. A crossroad. A coffee truck. An emergency vet. Yes.

Five years earlier, I'd been visiting some friends in the area. Harold was a mere youngster, sweet and diffident to other dogs. He was attacked at my friend's home by their dog, a tense night as the Granddad had died. Grief took over the home and the two dogs reacted. And Harold was so badly torn up, an artery bit open, that we flew up from Arlington late at night to the only emergency vet. I'd had to leave him there overnight, to be sewn back up. Although, I'd arrived during the night and slept in my truck outside, couldn't be parted from him, not completely.

This was the vet clinic. I stopped. Gave Harold a hug and walked inside.

"How can I help?" A young lady in white stood behind the counter. Her blond hair was tied in a tight bun, her face round and soft like a half-baked loaf of white bread. She put down her pen and focused fully on my story.

"Five years ago, a vet here saved my dog's life. I live in NM, and was just passing, a fluke really to recognize the place, but I had to stop, to say thank you. Thank you so much." The days of stress took a toll on me and I got pretty emotional, my voice quavering and eyes wet.

"Really? Oh, you know, no one ever comes back, not like that. Five years, you said? And you didn't know you'd drive past? That's amazing. Let me get the vet. Marianne! Come out here, I want you to meet someone."

She explained my story to the vet, and they looked Harold up on their records. "Oh, yes, it was touch and go for a minute. How is he?"

I pointed out the window and there in the front of

the van sat Harold and Rosie, tongues out, watching me happily in the morning cool. Grinning widely, Marianne, the vet and Stephanie, the tech, shook my hands, thanked me as I thanked them.

Warm Beach sounded just right. It was and it wasn't.

Driving down towards the beach, all the signs said loudly, No Parking! Residents Only! No Parking! I drove down an alley near the beach, glimpsing the ocean over those no-parking signs. Not so friendly here, that was obvious. Seeing someone walking her dog, I asked for help. She pointed back to the south where there was only one spot hidden behind other signs. She shrugged when I commented about the lack of welcome, but she did grin when Stevie popped up onto the dashboard.

"You're traveling with a cat? That's amazing! I've not seen that before, how wonderful. Yes dear, turn around here and head down the dead-end, you'll find a place to park. It's a little small but you'll just about make it in this. Have fun on the beach."

She was right, damn tight steep narrow one track that ended at two homes, both with the usual 'no parking dammit, can't you read?' signs. I turned around, ready for a quick retreat if necessary. A look around told me that we were alone. Doors open. Dogs out,

Stevie came out too, but only for a moment. Then it was time to grab a cat, throw him inside, and lock the doors. The open beach called. Dogs had to run.

A low grey cloud cover made the view dismal, damp and unappealing, yet it was the first beach Rosie had seen. She ran. Oh how she ran. Harold too, he ran back to the water, into the sea, drinking and spitting up salty water, chasing birds, running into me full pelt with Rosie on his heels, all because both were ecstatic. Wide smiles, tails low, full steam they ran and ran until I laughed so hard and fell onto the wet sand, uncaring, free at last. This was what I'd dreamed of. This moment was what we'd been driving towards. The freedom of the empty beaches, the seagulls, the overcast days, the smell and taste of salt on my lips, it was perfect. I forgot the shitty privacy signs. Forgot the ongoing stress of an unhappy van. The worries about my animals. The constant questions about what next, or where next. This. This was the moment that made it all worthwhile. This bleak lonely beach and two dogs playing hard in a damp morning one summer's day.

KAYAK POINT STATE PARK, WASHINGTON

I don't have a kayak.

There we were though, setting up for a late breakfast at the Kayak Point State Park, waiting for Dawn to arrive within an hour and I couldn't find out the origin of the name of the park though.

The day-use area was empty, with only one other vehicle by the entrance and so I'd driven to the far end, and parked next to a picnic table on the beach. Doors open. Dogs out. Stevie jumped down then froze mid-step.

"What's that smell? What are those birds flapping about on the water? Where the hell are we? Hawold? Hawold!"

Harry ran up to him and breathlessly explained beaches and sand and running and oh my, he had to run some more.

"Sand? Like in a litter box? The biggest litter-box in the world?" Stevie strode over to near Rosie and started to do the litter box scratch, sniff, scratch, then moved on another few feet to repeat the process. He did this for ten minutes before happily doing his business, while staring at the waves and the gulls. His fluffy white tail swished behind him as he wandered around the driftwood. "This is amazing! Can we stay?"

"Yep, at least for the next few days. Oh, someone's coming, you might want to hide." Three older people in sensible shoes slowly walked past us to the end of the parking lot before turning back, which was when they noticed all three critters. Stevie recognized the sound of someone wanting to pet him and he flew into the van and hid under the bed.

"A cat! I love cats! My name's JoAnn, no e. And you're traveling with a cat!" JoAnn was in her late fifties at least, with short cropped grey hair, baggy pants, and sparkling eyes. She made friends with Rosie first and then Harold, who exhausted by all the running around had decided to join us. The two friends were keeping Mattie company as the doctor had ordered her to walk for half an hour twice a day. She was indeed a large lady, puffing with exertion and goodwill.

"Have you been to the San Juan Islands? You really must go there. There are some wonderful campgrounds on the main island. The ferry goes every day, in fact it leaves here many times each day, oh you really must go. You'll not be sorry."

They wandered off. While drinking a hot chai with all the pets out dozing on the sandy beach, I looked it up: The State park on the San Juans was looking for camp hosts. Now there's an idea! With a quick hesitation, I applied online.

"I could live here," I muttered. One, two, three pets nodded in agreement. Okay then, we liked the coast.

Dawn! Oh Dawn! She flew out of her car and into my arms. Too long, five years since we'd seen each other last, and that was the year that Harold had ended up at the emergency vets. We hugged and laughed, and made fun of the grey hairs and how old we must be now...She's about 5 ft. 5", buzzed fair hair, adorably prominent ears, and the bluest of eyes that rarely stop twinkling. The life and soul of a happy heart, that's Dawn.

I sat her down at the table and made her chai, handing out some random snacks of fruit, cookies, cheese and crackers. We sat at the concrete picnic table on that blustery morning in Washington, and it was as if we were twenty-five again meeting up after a day away from each other. Nothing has changed: everything has changed. Life.

We put Stevie in the van and closed up shop before taking a hike with the pups down the driftwood-lined seaside. A handful of others walked, all smiling and bundled up in sweaters and hats. A thick evergreen forest covered the steep cliffs next to us, steps leading up to the campsite where we'd reserved a spot for two nights. A pier, three hundred feet long, had a sign announcing that the pups weren't welcome on there, probably a good thing as the seagulls had claimed it for themselves. Harold would have wanted to catch one, somehow, and determined to catch one, he'd have fallen off and into the sea. Not a good idea considering he couldn't swim in the calmest of lakes. The waves slapped against the beach as we walked underneath, chatting away, easy company. It was just so wonderful to see her again. Family.

Van Dreamy was acting up again. Not a good sign. I'd parked the damn vehicle in our campsite, opened a beer, and sat down amongst the pines and firs, watching Dawn set up her tent, or tried to.

"I don't remember! Sheesh, it's not been that long. Er? Any ideas there?"

"Hmm. Not really. Let's try it this way." I ambled over, picking up one of the poles. Five minutes later, "let's try it this other way then, shall we?"

The dogs watched, bellies full, and Stevie was asleep in the van with the doors closed. Finally Dawn got it up successfully despite my efforts and filled it with bedding. I'd set up a campfire for later, scrabbling around in the underbrush getting kindling and odds and ends together for us. So far, I'd only bought one pack of firewood and was pretty proud of my gathering abilities.

"Still cheap then eh?"

I laughed, "yep! Feel free to go buy us some from the host while you fill the water bucket for the dogs."

I sat back down to finish my beer, thankful for her company and toasted my sober pal with my bottle as she headed off with bucket in hand. Good friend.

Harold picked himself off the dirt and wandered over to the table. "I remember her. Did we stay with her sometime? It's all kinda foggy."

"We went up to see her for a day in Seattle. You were doped up on painkillers though. I'm surprised you recognize her."

"She smells good. I like her."

"Did I meet her?" Rosie piped up from her blanket.

"No, you weren't born yet. You like her though?"

"Oh yes, she scratches my back really well for a beginner. She doesn't have a dog, does she? It's okay; I like her anyway. Are we staying here tonight? With her?"

"Yep, and I have a surprise for you both later on. Some friends of yours want to see you."

"Really? Who?"

ARLINGTON, WASHINGTON

"Harold! Rosie!"

Two teenage girls squealed in delight. Rosie barked.

Harold ran rings around them, brushing against Claire, and the twins were trying to pet him in his frenzy. It didn't work.

"Me too! Me too!" Rosie wriggled around Claire and Dawn, begging for attention. The girls giggled and grabbed at the pups, trying to catch them, calm them down. It really didn't work. Dawn watched us with bright smiling eyes, but saying nothing. I'd forgotten to introduce her. Sorry about that.

"Oh right, weird to me as this is, you all haven't met each other yet, have you? This is Dawn, one of my first friends in the States; we met in Madison, what twenty-five years ago? This is Claire, Zoe and Katherine; we all lived next to each other in Madrid for the last eight years. Phil will be here with us later, right?"

Hugs, chatter, catching up, introducing, all as I hustled the pups back into Dawn's car. We'd left the van at the campsite as it was making those grinding wheel-falling-off noises. The restaurant set up a picnic table for six in the shade on the patio. Food ordered, beers to be drunk, some serious chatter began. To be honest, I zoned out, relaxed at having my family of friends around me. I didn't have to explain anything, excuse my travels, or tell them where I was from. This circle knew me the best.

"What are you thinking about there?" Claire woke

me up from the daydreams.

"I could live here, that's what I was thinking. The beaches, small towns, friendly people so far, mountains near by, I like it."

"Really? I'd love that!" Zoe, my sixteen-year-old friend was delighted. Kate grinned next to her, a slightly quieter twin, she usually let Zoe and I chat the most with an occasional comment to keep us on track. Both are incredibly smart kids, now teaching robotics to younger school kids after school.

"Yeah, why not? I'm tired of New Mexico. I think I'm suffocating in Madrid. I need a challenge."

Phil sat down and carried on as if he'd been hanging out with us the whole time. "There are companies that do that, you know? Pack and move everything. You wouldn't even have to go back if you didn't want to."

"I hate it here."

Claire stared out over the highway in front of us. Dawn had helped me drop off the van at a mechanic and Claire and I were having a last beer together before I carried on my travels, hopefully that is. "I truly hate it here." She added in emphasis.

During our conversation and Dawn's encouragement to move here, the chatter of the girls, and the practical information of Phil's, I hadn't noticed her silence the night before. Claire lit a cigarette now and breathed deeply before continuing.

"Don't do it. Not here. Maybe in Olympia or on the Islands, but not here. Arlington is full of church ladies, conservatives of the worst type; they even give me grief about my short hair. They constantly ask me why I don't go to church. They'd hate you, not married? No kids? Queer? No chance. Don't do it. Not here."

She looked so sad that I was shaken, taken aback, to see my close friend so lonely. She talked about her friends, or rather acquaintances, those people around her who just didn't understand her being a working artist. She had a studio that Dawn and I had visited in the morning, with Claire excitedly pulling out each piece, giving stories and processes behind each one. It was heart-warming to see her so excited about her work. Dawn asked all the right questions, genuinely interested, and open to spending time with us both at the Art Barn.

But then Dawn had gone back to Seattle, work called. We'd hugged, promised to stay in touch, especially since I was sure I'd be relocating to the Northwest within a year. We didn't know how soon we'd bump into each other again.

Arlington, Washington, is a small town, a conservative town, more like a suburb of the big city, with many commuting to work. It was also surrounded by agricultural land, with dairy farms and wineries, rivers, and the wilderness only a half hour away. And yes, churches stood on many a street corner. I liked it though; the downtown was friendly, full of small stores, cafes, and had a local's focus. We were sitting outside the Cedar Stump Brewery with dogs at my feet. It was a warehouse with a concrete yard. Of all the breweries I'd found so far, this had to be the ugliest but the beer hit the spot. For me anyway.

Claire sipped her IPA and asked if I were serious.

"Kinda. I need to move somewhere. But maybe not here?"

Claire laughed at that luckily. "Well, I'd visit you in Olympia if that helps? Come on, your van must be ready by now surely."

We downed our pints and packed the lounging dogs back into her car.

Kevin and Gerry were hunkered still under the van's front wheels when we parked in the shade of a nearby warehouse. Kevin stood up, wiping his hands. He was a skinny tall fella in loose blue coveralls, with his dark hair slicked back and a smile genuine and welcoming. He walked up with a grin.

"Well, it wasn't what we thought. But I did find that the ball joint had broken through the plate. We replaced all of that, I'm glad you gave me the go ahead, it made it quick and easy. Not too expensive for you either. I don't know if that's the noise you talked about though. We took it for a drive and didn't hear a knocking or clunking, nothing really. Well, let me show you. You're ready to go."

Claire said her goodbyes, kids and schools and packing to leave for Kentucky took her away. It made me sad though, to know how little at home she felt here. Deeply sad for my friend. But Van Dreamy was fixed! Or so we thought.

Kevin stood next to the van as I set up the dogs inside and closed it back up, grabbing my credit card and reading glasses. "Okay, I'm ready. What's the damage?"

ANACORTES, WASHINGTON

A familiar field. A shower. Laundry. Books from the free stack. A walk on the beach with the pups. Stevie out on a rope for a short walk. A beer at the restaurant overlooking the marina.

Van Dreamy was not fixed. Exactly the same bloody noises. Falling off wheels. Grinding metal on metal. Screeching. Clunking. Bloody horrible noises that hit after an hour on the road. I pulled off into a farm, reversed, a three point turn, forward and back twice, then back onto Highway 20 without a peep. Bloody horrible van.

The beer helped. It usually does. The sunset over hundreds of pristine sailboats of all sizes, the tinkling of the flagpoles in the breeze, a new book to read and a plan. It all helped. The security guard welcomed us back, took my twenty bucks, and promised to keep us safe overnight.

In the morning, we headed south after a quick detour to a park for a leash free roaming for all three pets. I'd sat on the step of the van, sipping my coffee and keeping an eye out for rangers. We hadn't yet been caught for the free-roaming activities, that was to come later.

The road wandered past the state park and across Deception Pass onto Whidbey Island. The highway meandered through open fields and small rural towns. We made great time and found Ebeys Landing State Park. We had a couple of hours to kill before the ferry, as yes we were taking a ferry! From Coupeville to Port Townsend on the Olympic Peninsula for less than twenty dollars. Hell yeah, I couldn't wait. I love ferries; they remind me of being a kid and crossing the English Channel, with Mum and I on the front with the wind

slapping us merrily as we'd sing together. Yep, I love
ferries, and even better, it meant I didn't have to drive
through Seattle. In theory the ferry is just an extension
of Highway 20, and would bring us out on Highway
101.

I let the critters out and we clambered over and
around the piles of driftwood, the timbers that spread
out along a mile of beach facing Canada. We were so
close, but I never did take us across. Next time. We'll
go next time.

Stevie ran hard after Rosie, his tail high when
walking back towards me, happy to be free. "I like this.
Can we stay here? Please? That place last night wasn't
nice. I'm a tiger and we have to run every day! Every
day! Okay? Okay, thanks, I'm getting inside now. I'm
tired."

Rosie ran after Harold who in his chase mode found
himself knee-deep in the ocean. He stood there, shocked
for a moment, looked at me, and ran back to solid
ground as fast as possible. Shaking it off, he laughed as
Rosie did exactly the same. "She doesn't learn, does
she?"

"No, but that's what makes us laugh, isn't it? That
she just doesn't care? Silly bugger she is. Yes, you!
Come here Rosie, let's get ready for a ferry ride."

"What's a ferry?" Stevie popped up from under the

bed? "Will I like it?"

"Can I lick it?" Rosie shook herself dry before claiming the front seat.

"Can I eat it?"

OLYMPIC PENINSULA, WASHINGTON

I hated it.

OLYMPIC PENINSULA, WASHINGTON

Okay, not completely, but I kinda hated it. Dense forests, small conservative rural towns, Trump signs everywhere, more trees, then more trees, thick understory and everywhere up high loitered hungry bald eagles, eyeing up my little tiger. Stevie was oblivious, all he knew was that he'd be let out for a walk only to be suddenly grabbed and thrown back inside Van Clunky. Oh, yes, Van Clunky was killing my good mood. Bugger it.

We passed four campgrounds; all were full this Saturday afternoon. I'd known it. I'd expected it but this was the first time in however many miles we'd driven that I really had no clue as to where we'd stay the night. Mid-afternoon, Hwy 101 headed west to the furthest western point with us stopping at a few beaches on the way to nowhere. The sea breeze blew away the crankiness and we hiked, that is the dogs and I. Stevie had to stay inside, eagles sniffed him out within minutes the few times the bugger walked on the sand with us. The sea salt in the air had my licking my lips, craving fish and chips, but it was yet another peanut butter sandwich instead. The cool damp warmth of summer on the Puget Sound reminded me of holidays in Wales as a kid, happy memories.

I could live here.

From my notes, there were three free campgrounds, slightly off the only two highways, all along forest roads but did I find them? Not a chance, the dense woods on either side of the highway became claustrophobic and I saw nothing but a fork in the road. Southwest towards Ozette Lake or Northwest to Neah Bay? For no good reason, we took the Hoko-Ozette Road, towards a lake and another campground. First though, I pulled off and parked behind a huge gravel pile on that narrow empty two-lane road. With such a deserted place, it felt safe for us all to walk, pee, and have a break from a full day's travel.

Then a Volvo pulled up. Fuck. Seriously? Can't I

get any alone time? I flagged them to slow down as I grabbed the tiger and wrestled him back into the van. Fuck. Why here? Why now?

"HAROLD!"

A door opened, a yell, and Dawn emerged with arms out, laughing and squealing in amazement as someone else climbed out the other side.

"This is Annie! Annie, it's Sleam. And Harold! I recognized Harold and the front of the van. I made her back up! I can't freakin' believe it! What the hell are you doing here?" She grabbed me in a bear hug and spun us around. Rosie bounced around, jumped in the Volvo, and watched from the driver's seat, tongue hanging low.

"What the hell are you doing here? Where are we anyway? I can't believe it! How on earth? Incredible...incredible!"

The three of us stood there amazed. In the middle of the Olympic Mountains, we ran in to each other, how on earth?

"Where are you going?" Annie passed me a bottle of water. "We're looking for a campground but they're all full. What about you?"

I told of my afternoon looking for a place on the north coast, and that "the last resort is one more campground at Lake Ozette, it's small and out of the way so I'm hoping not many people know of it. Want to go claim a space for us? I bet you drive faster than me."

"There's bound to be a place, how couldn't there? It's meant to be, right? We have to camp together!" Dawn tempted Rosie back out of the car and over to me before agreeing to save us a place. They drove off. Stevie came back out cursing tourists.

"No, it's our friend! Dawn and someone who smells of dogs." Rosie licked her lips.

"Oh great, another dog-lover. What about me?"

Walking around the dirt pile and back to the van, I told them we'd be camping together in the trees next to a lake. I chatted away, the kids following me along. I stepped inside. They stood and stared at me, not climbing up until I said the magic words:

"Anyone hungry?"

"Is that a site?" Annie, a thirty-something Seattle native in baggy black pants and a soft grey sweatshirt walked through the old growth trees, shaking her head. "I can't tell. Let's keep going."

We did another lap and came back to the same parking area. A picnic table, a fire-ring, and flattened grass.

"Yep, we found the last one, shit, that's lucky! I can't imagine driving any more today. Quick, go get the

Volvo, Annie. We'll save the place and then Sleam can go get the van after that. We can't lose it now, right?" Dawn grabbed one of the dog leashes and sat at the table, "Yep, home for the night. Where are the toilets?"

A kayaker slowly drifted past on the glassy lake as we sat and enjoyed a crystal blue sky turning mauve as the sun set behind the spruce, cedars, and alders. We'd walked the short path through salmonberries, huckleberries, and lush ferns. The dogs sniffed happily, peeing on every other shrub and surprising quite a few ducks in the process much to Harold's delight. The air was mild but still a fire sounded just right, but not yet, not yet, sitting on a sandy beach beside this placid lake was too good to rush.

In order to get to Rialto Beach the next morning, we'd had to backtrack up to Highway 112, head south on Hwy 113 to Sappho, which was quite a photo opportunity at the sign for Old Sappho, and then further southwest to Mora and La Push. Again, one of the last campsites, but that time in a campground with 92 sites, crazy eh? Weekends on the peninsula were stupidly busy in July apparently. Tall cedar and pine trees circled our camp giving us privacy and places for Stevie to explore. Nervously I let him out, hungry, and watched the conifer's tree tips for eagles. Ravens found the boy instead, screeching, dive-bombing him, and scaring him back from the tree trunks to under the camper. Little Stevie sat there, muttering but for once not blaming me. At least he wasn't on a rope, unlike Rosie the White Wanderer.

We set up camp and then headed out for Rialto Beach, a place Dawn knew.

"This is why you need to move here, look at you! You haven't stopped grinning!" Dawn then explained to Annie about the night in Arlington, playing with the idea of my moving out here, perhaps just staying in Washington and not even going back to New Mexico as planned. That was her vote anyways.

"Really? That's great, I'd love to have you around. Dawn talks about you often enough, it's like I know you already. You'd find work pretty easily in the cities, especially if you stayed with TJs. There's one in Olympia you could check out."

We wandered along the beach, clambering over the driftwood; piled so high it was a scramble to keep up with the pups. The wind battered us, the waves slammed against the sand and boulders, and finally I had reached the Pacific Ocean. Yes, I couldn't stop grinning. This was the reason for the rush over the last weeks, a need to be on the coast, with sea-salted air in my hair, a glorious stickiness of skin, the damp cool afternoons, I couldn't be happier. Annie and Dawn were holding hands and giggling as they explored the rocks ahead of me. Amazing. So amazing.

CAPE DISAPPOINTMENT, WASHINGTON

No privacy, busy campground, noisy, kids, dogs, people everywhere, but no, it wasn't a disappointment. Stevie was on lockdown, a reluctant kitty in a crate, and the dogs and I guiltily loved it. Through the trees, past sand dunes, the beach opened up before us, so huge that it felt deserted despite people walking all over, kids playing in the waves. To the left, the beach reached for miles to a lighthouse, and with the dogs free to run, I followed them with sandals in hand, grinning widely. The seaside, the salty air, splashing waves; warm damp temperatures bring out such a stupidly happy side of me, pure child delight. I walked and walked, paddling in the ocean, splashing water on my face and neck, calling to the pups whenever other dogs were running around. I sat on the sand and stared at the slowly setting July sun. Perfection. Costly mind, more than had been spent at a single campground, but it's a State Park on the Pacific Coast. But $45 for one night? Yikes.

We'd driven all down the Olympic Peninsula on Highway 101, but apart from a few stops at empty beaches, I didn't like it. The signs for the coming presidency showed that my politics were unwanted there. I kept to myself, not even needing gas, so we kept going, trying to get out a claustrophobic rain forest.

Now *that* was the disappointment. It's the reason this part of Washington left a bad taste. I'd had such high hopes as so many friends had recommended the area to me, saying that the people, mountains, and ocean, all of it would suit me down to the sand in the toes. It didn't. The appeal was clear but apart from those hours spent on sand, the goal was to escape. I needed to get away to Oregon. Why there? It was the next place on my list of new home states, a place that might fit me. After the Olympic Peninsula, my mood crashed, and it was only the desire of finding a community, a landing point in Oregon, that kept me from crying.

Driving out of the park in the morning, the van began again: crunch, grind, crack, and clunk clunk. I hit my head on the steering wheel, muttering to myself. The critters said little. Stevie came over and sat on the dashboard, looking at me and then noticed the seagulls outside.

"Dammit. Okay, big dogs out, little dog in." Yes,

Stevie knew the difference. We got out and walked up to a fella in a big Ford truck with Washington plates.

"Hi, how are you? Any chance you can recommend a mechanic for me? Front wheel problems, I'm thinking."

The big man leaned out of the window and commiserated with me while writing down a number with surprisingly delicate handwriting. "Tell him Dan gave you the number. He's out of the business but he helps us out when we need advice if nothing else. I think it's a $40 call out fee though. Do you have any cash? I doubt he'd take a check."

Ron arrived in a broke down rust bucket, spluttering black smoke. "You got cash?"

Nodding, I started up and drove around the parking lot past a Game and Fish warden who was counting fishing boats on their way out to sea. Van Dreamy drove like a ghost, not a sound made. Nothing. Bitch. The dogs kept quiet. Even Stevie didn't make any complaints and Rosie quit joking around. Silent inside and out. Fuck.

"Well, I didn't hear a thing. You should be fine. That'll be $40."

"Could you at least look under there? See if you find anything loose?"

"I suppose so." And he levered himself out of his car, all three hundred and fifty pounds, huffing and wheezing. "I got health issues."

No kidding. I nodded sympathetically though as he lay down and poked around underneath, swearing to himself.

"Nope, can't see anything wrong. You might want to go see my friends in town, they've got a shop on the main street, been there forty years. Good family business. They could lift it up, check the driveshaft, that's what I'm thinking it is. Maybe. That'll be $40. You got cash?"

A sandy strip full of trees lined Seaview from the ocean and walking with the dogs on leashes in that morning sun on the way to the beach warmed us nicely.

Jonathon Stout first settled Seaview in 1880 when he purchased 153 acres to build a resort. People arrived by boat along the Columbia River and then horse and cart, quite a trek to get here. After a railroad built tracks along the peninsula, families came from Portland in the hundreds during the 1890s. These days the population hovers around 500 with tourism filling in hugely over summer.

Brandon, the owner in his early sixties, told me to give the mechanics a couple of hours and so I'd locked

Stevie in the big soft crate, told them to be careful not to scare the tiger in the back, and we'd wandered off to explore. For a summer's day in July, no one was around; it was truly deserted with only a huge expanse of packed sand and piled driftwood that appears during winter storms. Harold chased seagulls, even into the waves, not his favorite place to be but he lost himself in the game. The birds played with him too, zipping in and out of range, taunting and teasing the big black dog as he barked, wagged and ran. Rosie, my silly girl, dug holes, deep tunnels with only her bum sticking out. Her head would pop up every so often as she checked on me, sitting a hundred yards away soaking up the sunshine.

"Lovely dogs, aren't they?"

A compact elderly lady in sweats stood admiring the playing pups. Her hair was tied in a tight bun, her eyes a deep amber shone and her voice warmed to the topic. "My poodle, Betsy, died last summer. I can't get another, not knowing how many more days I'll wake up. Each day is a blessing. Are you visiting us?"

"Well, it wasn't planned but I'm glad it worked out that way." I explained about the mechanic, the van, and our trip.

"With a cat? Now that's unique, not often do you see that happen. When my husband and I moved here from Oklahoma, we brought the dog and the cat. The cat's not happy here though; he has to be an indoor cat, too many eagles and predators around. Do you keep yours in the van?"

"Mostly, he gets to walk with us but it depends where we are, whose around, that kind of thing. I don't know how it will be here on the coast, more people than we're used to. We'll see. I like it here though."

"Us too. Don plays in a local jazz band, I work at the library. It's a good place. Cheap houses. Nice people. Not too right wing, but there sure are a lot of churches once you get out of Seaview and drive up Long Beach. I'm not one to judge, but I don't like them Baptists."

And with that, she shook my hand and wandered off. Rosie's bum stuck out of a tunnel to China and Harold had collapsed on the dunes behind me.

"We couldn't find anything wrong. Well, just a small detail that rattled around in the engine but it needed to be fixed before it wrecked the radiator. That'll be $185. Come on back though if it happens again, okay? It was nice to meet you!"

As soon as we were out of sight, Van Dreamy morphed back into Van Clunky. I just couldn't go straight back, too much, too drained and in need of a break from thinking about it. I pulled onto the sand and with no one around, let Stevie enjoy the mile long litter box. He played with the insects in the sand dunes. I made sandwiches and a cup of tea. The dogs slept in the shade.

Back on the main road later that afternoon, Van Clunky and I slowly passed the mechanic shop, honking my horn, and they all looked up. Mick ran over and jumped in the front seat, displacing a sleeping white dog. She didn't complain though. Mick grinned and listened.

"Got it! Try turning around up here, and we'll go back. I know exactly what it is."

Back at the shop, we drove up and parked in the shade. Mick jumped out as Stevie climbed into his crate muttering away.

"Wheel bearings! I don't know why it would come and go like that; they never do that. They either go out or don't. None of this on and off grinding sound. Let's see, shall we?"

Mick reminded me of a skinny and wired speed freak from Madrid, NM that I knew, all weathered skin, big smile, chatting constantly. Mick grabbed tools, jacked up the van, and took off the wheel and parts. Out fell six shards of metal, the ball bearings, broken and torn by a few weeks of destruction.

"You're lucky it didn't catch fire!" he pronounced happily.

Right. Great. An hour later, we were ready to leave for Oregon. But first:

"That'll be $159 please."

PACIFIC CITY, OREGON

"Do you need help?"

Their sedan was deeply entrenched in soft sand. My question was redundant, I know, but was I meant to just assume they wanted my help? Sorry, I'm too English for that, we say sorry a lot and ask stupid questions if we can.

A family clambered out, sheepish, all six of them, two women in their thirties, typical jock types with the hair pulled back tightly and wearing spandex over their oh-so-white legs. The four kids bounced around in colorful summer shorts and tee shirts despite the chill wind. Aimlessly kicking sand at each other, the kids soon got bored and whiny.

"Can we play in the sand, Mom? Please?" The oldest at eight or nine pulled out her little plastic spade and bucket.

"Yes, but we need that," said Mom, grabbing the

twelve inches of plastic shovel. "Don't go far. And, yes, we'd love some help, thanks."

Soon there were another couple of families, myself, the kids and finally a couple Oregon State Park Rangers gathered around. What had this family been thinking when they drove a ten-year-old sedan into a sand bank? Didn't they think? I suppose not. The sand climbed up a steep short hill before heading onto a huge and deserted beach (relatively speaking). Grass stumps waved in the breeze as the kids ran circles around us, those of us with shovels of our own who were digging out the wheels of this two-wheel drive Honda. What were they thinking? It became my mantra while in Pacific City. Each and every day, I dug out another car or truck. That comes later though, this was my first morning in town and I liked it, the easy camaraderie, helping each other out, chatting and laughing together. I took a break and talked to Ranger James and Ranger Shannon. The fella was a new kid, all keen to help, but Shannon held back, shaking her head at the idiocy of drivers.

"It happens all the time. When I first started here, I'd offer to help dig, just like James here, but now? It's all I'd end up doing if I didn't step away. You see the Portlanders heading to the beach for the first time, seeing the tracks and just heading out to sea. Few make it. They don't notice that the ones who do park on the beaches are in four wheel trucks and Jeeps, you see. Sea-blindness I call it. Stupidity my boss calls it. Well, anyway, how are you?"

She took off her sunglasses and hat for a moment, and I saw myself in her. Blue eyes, weathered skin, short hair, healthy looking. I saw myself as a Ranger. It was an epiphany. I didn't tell her though, just explained about the trip, camping, and hoping to park near sand if not on it.

Shannon grinned, "Well, there is a parking area on a hard-packed beach up the road by the Pelican. Heard of it? The local microbrewery has a deck on the beach next to the dory fishing boats. You should check it out. It's pretty amazing to sit with your feet up on the railing, only a yard away from this expanse of sand, waves, wind, and tourists. I go there after work when I can, it's a favorite with locals too. Anyway, we must be going. James, put the shovel down! We've got to check on the Bob Straub Park before too long. Oh, you should check that one out. It's got awesome beach access and few people. The dogs will love it!"

We did. We loved it. The photos of us in the sands show two long doggy tongues and a widely smiling self. Blue skies, bare beaches, miles of dunes and the Pacific Ocean uncluttered by boats or even clouds, it was incredible. At the Park entrance, I'd worried that a Ranger would be on guard, checking on my critters because of the leash laws, but no. Five other cars and trucks lined up in a parking lot made for fifty or more. I settled us at one end, out of the way yet next to the trees, paths, and the empty sand dunes. With doors open, Stevie explored, pooped, climbed trees and hid under the van whenever a raven bothered him.

"I like it here, can we stay? There's a mouse in that grass, I just know it. I'll get it for you, honest! This is great, just what I needed." Stevie hunched down behind a blade of grass to watch a small hole under the tree nearest us. He hummed to himself, a perfect purr of contentment. I sat on the step into the van, and drank a cold mineral water and finished up with an apple and orange. The dogs had run so hard chasing seagulls that both were conked out inside. Relaxed, and unworried, I'd stopped looking for a ranger until Mike appeared.

"Is that your cat?"

We both looked to see Stevie watching from high in a branch, grey tail swishing nervously. "Yep. He's with us."

"You'd better be careful, I don't mind him wandering around, but there are eagles along this coast line, worse at dusk and dawn, but still. Be careful. I'd hate for you to lose him."

Assistant Ranger Mike as the label said, was in his late fifties, with clear skin, olive eyes, and a deep green uniform. I like uniforms; again, it's an English thing.

"How do you like your job? I'm thinking of applying," I blurted out. (I am? Oh, okay, I am.)

"You are? Oh, okay, you are serious? Well, it's great. I love it to be honest. I got burnt out on the office job, sold the business and hit the road for a year before settling here one summer. I love being outside all day long, and it's pretty mindless work in that I just clean up, check on the day parks, help visitors and that kind of thing. Then I go home and relax at night. It's seasonal, a union job too, so it's pretty well paid considering." He scratched at his beard, a short grey beard, and looked around. "This is pretty typical of the places I tend to. Not bad eh? If I wanted I could transfer for another position for a winter job, but I like the six months on, six off."

"That works for me." I told him of my landscaping business, writing, traveling, and he admitted to having no practical experience before applying.

"You'd be fine, in fact I think Nehalem Bay State Park is looking for an Assistant Ranger. Look it up if you get a chance. Well, good luck, maybe I'll see you around. And keep an eye out for the hawks as well."

He shook my hand and wandered off, checking the

trashcans, chatting to other families. But then he turned back, writing something down on his notebook. Uh oh. A ticket for the cat? After being so friendly? Nope, his telephone number.

"Just in case you want to talk more."

Pacific City is a small little visited coastal town, near Tillamook, the Dairy capitol of Oregon. I liked it, one main street, a stop sign, a bar, bakery, thrift store, and homes scattered against the hill eastwards overlooking the ocean. I really liked it. Driving around one morning, we'd found the Grateful Bread Bakery, and inside was packed, with a line of more families waiting outside for a table. I headed to the counter instead and chatted to Emily, a transplant from the east coast by her accent. A homemade cranberry scone and large coffee with cream cost me $2.75. Incredible. And tasty.

Pacific City, Oregon: elevation 13 feet. It's pretty funny to me coming from the Ortiz Mountains in New Mexico that anyone would pronounce such an elevation as thirteen feet. Anyway, the history lesson for you: In the 1850s a huge wild fire in the Willamette Valley forced the local Native American tribes to flee the area by boat, and the fire decimated their hunting grounds, farmland and killing much of the old growth forests, leaving them to subsist mostly by fishing. In 1876 all two hundred in the tribe were forcibly relocated to a reservation south of the bay and 'settlers' claimed the area for themselves. In 1886, a salmon cannery was built in Nestucca Bay, which heralded a prosperous time of fishing, logging, and dairy farming in the valley, and along the rich arable land oceanside. With a failing commercial salmon cannery, the Dory Fleet came into their own with double ended boats that are launched from the sandy beaches directly into the ocean, and it's become a focus and pride of locals to fish with dory boats these days. The current population was estimated at around a thousand with many a tourist owning second homes and shares in the numerous condos at Cape Kiwanda. PC though is very much a rural small town and local focused even as it was friendly to visitors like myself. With BLM on three sides and the ocean on the fourth, there is limited growth possible. As such the home prices were not aimed at people like me being hundreds of thousands for 600 ft cottages with a view, way out of my range. I did daydream though as we drove up and down the hillside: I could image living in a place like that, it reminded me, yes, of Wales. Dark grey cloud cover came and went, and like in Wales the locals were holding on to their homes despite a need for the tourist dollars, and those four miles of broad beaches at Bob's just welcomed me home as it were.

The Pelican Microbrewery was my new favorite pub in the world. How could it not be? It offered me home brewed award winning beers made on site, with huge windows and a large outdoor patio and deck that lead onto sandy beaches overlooking dunes, dory boats, tide pools and the Haystack rock. The sun set, a glowing orb in a clear blue evening sky. My beer was chilled and my feet propped on an empty chair as I watched the day come to an end. Quite a first day and even though I didn't know where we would set up camp, I didn't care for once. This was too freaking awesome to leave.

I could live here. Work here. Drink here. Yep, what a place for me. The critters were all pooped from running wild in the dunes with me morning and afternoon. They slept deeply inside as I sat next to a campfire in Sand Lake, an aptly named National Forest campground ten miles north of town. The trees surrounded us, the dunes spread out for miles around us, and that was why this campground existed here, miles from anywhere, but cheap and that I liked. A thousand acres were set aside for dune recreation, for those playing on ATVs, bikes, and OHVs of all kinds. Luckily, these same people sleep in as I discovered, all day long you'd hear the mosquito buzzing in the trees and beyond in the dunes around me. I'd set up camp off to the side, making sure that we weren't on any through-route and under a couple of trees for Little Stevie who'd become quite the climber. It made sense since at home we only had ten-foot tall junipers and nothing more. He loved this trip for the trees if nothing else. At least, he'd stopped complaining. Harold's only complaint? That he couldn't catch the gulls. Rosie? She is such a dog; she loved everything, no question. Curled tail held high, brown patch over one eye, her compact white furry body attracted many a complement and she was beginning to like strangers more and more, mostly as a source of snacks and strokes. Their wanting photographs of her worked well as she knew to stop still when a camera was held up. A good model she is.

Yep, I could work for the State Parks. How had I not thought of this before? Given my landscaping business, the practical skills from building my own home, and knowing about bookkeeping from being self-employed, I had the requirements listed on the OSP website. Yes, I'd checked after talking to Assistant Ranger Mike. But no, I didn't call him. He had got me thinking though, and finally I understood that it really was possible for me to find good work, good outdoor work, near the ocean. It couldn't get much better than that in my book.

"Hmm…I'll apply and see what happens. What do you think, kids? Live in Oregon for a while?"

Tails wagged from inside the van (I heard the thumps) and Stevie wandered back over to see if his dinner was ready, purring and exhausted from playing all day.

"I'm hungwy!" He popped inside and looked for his bowl on the dashboard. I closed the door behind him and relaxed next to the fire until the beer stopped flowing. Pretty late.

Driving around the next morning I whispered to myself, 'welcome home' and grinned widely. A timid sun peaked from behind a few wispy clouds over a grey ocean. Working for the Parks filled my mind, how obvious, how perfect it seemed. Internet was next then, a café for me to make as an office while applying for jobs and to upload my latest articles. Cape Kiwanda is an odd place but likeable. It was full of RV parking, high-end homes and condos, but there was also a dory fleet on the beach, the Pelican Brewery and yes a café with Internet. I settled in after taking the pups peeing, I mean 'walking' around the vacation homes. Not a bad start to staying in the area, I posted my resume on the Oregon State Parks and sipped a latte. Seasonal well-paid work on the Pacific Ocean, fuck yeah. I can do that. I put it slightly better on my cover letter but it was dominating my thoughts. Good dreams, wide smiles, and caffeine rushing through me, it was time to walk the dogs along four miles of barren dunes. Again.

TILLAMOOK, OREGON

"The Land Of Cheese, Trees and Ocean Breeze."

So says the official Tillamook County website. I never did get into the Tillamook Cheese Factory, mostly because I told myself it's not going anywhere and since I'm moving to the region, there wasn't a rush. I drove past, looking for a bank, grocery store, thrift store, and a carwash with vacuum. The van was a mess. Weeks, no months on the road with three furry four-leggeds in there had built up quite some dander, not too mention a smell of unwashed paws. Spilling the pee-jug on the rug hadn't helped any.

I blame the Pelican Brewery. Three beers on their beach patio one afternoon, that and the conversation with Sandy and her boyfriend, Vernon. They were in their late forties; she was skinny and hyper, a nervous habit of flicking shoulder length brown hair out of her face as if it annoyed her. Vernon was softer, an indoor dog if you know what I mean, with soft clean manicured hands and a pleasant if teasing nature. They joined me at the bar, chatting about the darkening sky that afternoon. They worked together in Portland, office jobs so I had little to add to that conversation, but then Sandy told me it was her birthday and that they'd come to Cape Kiwanda for a weekend together before she went to Bend to be with the family. Her fiftieth birthday, a big deal, and one she didn't like the idea of at all. She kept asking for reassurance that you couldn't tell, could you? I told her that it would be my fiftieth next year, and she didn't look surprised. I lost interest at that point. No, actually, I worked it more. They paid for my beers. Three beers and the Pelican is not a cheap place. Sandy walked off to the bathroom as Vernon and I claimed a table outside.

"The family birthday? It's an intervention. They're worried about her drinking. She drinks a lot, and then? Well, she gets kinda shitty with people, strangers mostly." He grinned sheepishly. "I backed out, couldn't face going there knowing about the ambush. Don't say anything, okay? Do you want to stay for dinner? My treat? No, you have to go, what right now? Your dogs you say? Oh right, okay then. I'll say goodbye for you. Are you sure?"

Down the road, I pulled off at Tierra Del Mar beach, a place I'd found on my wanderings. Even better than Bob's park, we parked there during the day on the hard-packed sand near the entrance. With the doors open, the view was of ocean and cliffs to the south. Incredible. Well, that night, after escaping Sandy and Vernon, I stopped for the first time at sunset. Even better. Only three other vehicles. I claimed our usual viewing spot and let the critters roam as I peed in a bucket inside Van Dreamy. Walking around with an empty bladder was so much better. Harold came running up excitedly.

"There's a really nice couple next door. They gave us treats. Even Stevie! They've got a cooler and everything. You should come with me. Rosie's camped out at the woman's feet. She wouldn't come back with me! Stevie, er, Stevie's in the dunes again, stalking a fly. Come on! Hurry up!" He bounded around the van and disappeared again. I followed to find Rosie lying belly up as a woman was scratching and cooing over her soft coat. Oops.

"Hi, sorry about that. Rosie! Come on, don't bother these people."

Rosie rolled over but didn't come. She looked at the couple and their cooler, her meaning clear. "I'm hungry and you smell of beer again. I'm staying. Unless? You have treats too?"

The couple stood up and shook my hand as I frowned at Rosie. Harold was standing next to me, wagging softly, hoping for more of the good stuff.

"We're Maisy and Ken. Come on over, we've got

snacks, it's a perfect time for the sunset. And your animals are adorable! Here you go, brie and crackers okay to start with? Ken, get the salmon will you, dear? Here you are, beer from the Pelican or a cocktail? Rum and coke goes so perfectly with the sunshine and the beach, don't you think?"

Ken pulled out another folding chair for me and handed over a plate of salmon, brie, tomatoes, and crackers. He wasn't much taller than me with a short dark buzz cut and bushy beard. Maisy mixed up a strong rum and coke, a full figured woman in her sixties, she chatted away, asking about the trip, my plans and of course the cat. I sat happily answering as much as needed before another question popped up. Stevie peeked out from under the van, trying to get me to feed him, but that could wait. Their food was really good. Really good. After a couple of refills, I staggered back to the van and fed the critters, and as I closed the door, knocked over the pee-bucket. Swearing under my breath, I threw a towel on the mess and left it to soak up. Maisy had just pulled out some chocolate, and it called my name.

"If you go through Idaho, be careful of all the wild fires near Boise. That mountain pass is closed I believe. It's damn hot this time of year anyway. I don't recommend it. Have you been south yet? To Bandon?

Coos bay? Anywhere down there? Oh, there's a great little campground near Bastendorff Beach worth visiting. It's a busy one, but free if I remember rightly. Didn't we go there one year Maise? I thought so. We have an RV now though so we tend to go to places with full hook-ups. I did like that area. We're from Spokane. Oh you passed through there? A good city, the military does right by us. Keeps the locals in work, supply and demand you see."

Ken talked easily as he prepped more food for us women folk. The conversation flowed from tales of one campground to another, places we'd both visited. We watched cars drive onto the soft sand, watched them push themselves out again: Television beach style. The sun set finally and off they went, but first telling me to stay on the beach overnight.

"No one cares, not really. If you set up a tent and built a platform, perhaps! But no, in a van? Stay, you'll love being here on your own. It's wonderful at sunrise. Just wait and see! And here's some fish for the cat. We bought it at Wal-Mart in Tillamook."

Tillamook. I liked it. We drove around the downtown one-way systems, back onto the main drag, in and out of side roads. With the errands done easily, a clean van, sleepy critters, it was a nice change to explore for the sake of curiosity. Most of this trip, we'd been going onto the next town, a new campground, an errand to be done, but rarely had I simply wandered aimlessly in a small city like this. Was it because of the email I'd gotten? My application to the Oregon State Parks had been accepted. Next stage, a review and references to be checked. It had been accepted! This might actually happen! There had been a posting for an Assistant Park Ranger needed at Nehalem Bay State Park; I'd applied online. Easy. Even with a hangover. Now then, a day later, no the next morning, I'd received notice that they were considering me for the position. Time to check out Nehalem Bay then.

We spent a leisurely morning in and around Tillamook, chatting to the Guatemalan cashier at the thrift store. I'd made her day and mine by knowing her town, San Pedro, on Lake Atitlan, telling her of working in another village near hers some years ago in 2005. She gabbled away in Spanish and told me how she'd been there at that time too. Small world. I shook her hand, loving talking to her, thanking her for a warm welcome to the area. I walked out smiling with a new pair of boots, putting them on at the door as mine had fallen apart with months of hard wearing. Stuffing the old ones into the trashcan, nodding at the customers coming in, my hope for a new future filled me and I skipped over to the van, bounced inside and handed out treats for no reason.

NEHALEM BAY, OREGON

"Do you mind if I just look around? I've applied for a job here and…"

The ranger standing at the entrance, taking money, grinned and sent me through without paying a dollar. He passed over a map, as the place was big enough for three separate loops and 265 campsites. Shit, that's a lot. There was even a horse-camp and another set aside for cyclists and their tents. The main campground followed the curve of a sand dune barrier between ocean and hillside. A flat meadow for some RVs and a winding loop or three for the rest of the tents, trailers, and campers like mine. Driving around, signs pointed to a two-mile hiking trail, another for a six-mile horse trail, fishing access, and kid-friendly beaches. Then we passed a low and large shower building for women. I parked quickly in the shade and walked in as if belonging. A long hot free shower was incredible. I remembered this ploy for the rest of the trip, asking to look around the larger campgrounds, finding the trash and recycling, and finishing with a hot shower. My day was complete. The state park was okay, it didn't inspire me to be honest, but hey, if I got a job, I'd be more than happy to work next to the ocean. Where would we live though? That worried me. Would they provide housing? Even with three pets? Or would I have to pay the summer rental rates?

We headed back to Tierra Del Mar beach for another quiet night watching a sunset and sunrise. For free. Not a bad life.

Another day, another car stuck in sand. It averaged out to two per day, time for me to pull out the shovel, wander over shaking my head to dig out the back wheels and heave-ho, back they'd go. I didn't mind. It was something to do while watching waves for hours on end. Time to hit the road again perhaps? Was I getting bored? Yeah, kind of. I wrote in the sand with my finger, thank you, and packed up for the next adventure.

PORT ORFORD, OREGON

The best fish and chips since leaving Britain: Head over to the Crazy Norwegian's Place on Highway 101. Perfectly crisp batter, melting cod, chunky fries with enough for leftovers and it only cost me $13. Well worth it. I sat in the van overlooking the port, a most unusual one by far. It took me a while to work out what was different. The boats, all kinds of boats, were high above the water on a concrete platform with two cranes pulling them out of the ocean. Fascinated, I waited to see one being lifted but never timed it right. We'd camped up the road by a creek in a small NF campground; at the far end of the meadow was an unclaimed spot with huge trees for Stevie and a creek for the pups. A table for me became the kitchen and for a few days I played with some fancier meals. The fish and chips weren't planned. The sign caught my attention during that evening's exploration.

The Crazy Norwegian's was a locals' place; you could tell by the way each table greeted each other, asking about Mary's hips, the current fishing, and of course the weather. I waited for my to-go order and wished they'd include me. All of the people I'd met so far on the trip were all transplants, rarely a long-term local. What does it take to open up to visitors like myself? I had questions, but not the desire to make them answer me and so left with a bag of goodies and wandered back to the dock quietly. Talk to the dogs again.

"Is that cod? Oohh, can I have some?" Stevie sat only inches from the plate. "Please?"

Port Orford had been on my list of places to visit for being smaller, artistic, individualistic, and on the coast, with less of obvious tourism, and offering more of a plain oceanside without kitsch. In 1792, Vancouver, an explorer, landed and met a local tribe, the Tututni Peoples, describing them as 'mild and peaceable.' However in 1850, the US Congress put into force the Oregon Land Donation Act, which allowed white settlers to claim land even though the Native Americans had signed no such agreement. As you can guess, it ended in blood, fighting drawn out until the locals were outnumbered and forced to relocate to Northern Oregon onto a newly formed reservation. After, or rather during that time, gold had been discovered. Do you think there is a link? Nah, nor me.

EDSON CREEK CAMPGROUND, OREGON

"Hi! Hi! My name's Kitty Lee Nelson. I was born when my grandma died. I'm pushing my little brother." The little seven year old walked past my camper van in her matching peach colored tee shirt and shorts, full of songs. Her brother stared at me blandly.

Stevie had a blast, hanging out in the trees surrounding us, sitting up high and only coming down if

I walked up the road. Then he'd fling himself down the trunk and bound up to Harold, jumping on the poor sensitive big dog to make him squeal yet again. It really did work every time. Those boys. Rosie splashed in the stream for hours, she was catching fish was her excuse but did she bring us dinner? Nope. Harold lay on the grass, leaning against me as I read and researched more places to visit. The campsite was so cheap and relaxed for us all that it became home base for a week. Lazy mornings, then off to explore we'd go, although Stevie thought he'd prefer to stay alone until I started up the van…funny that.

Driving to Bandon one day I glanced in the rear view mirror. Stevie, on a leash as usual so he can't jump out a window or door, well, he was innocently lying on his upper shelf. Harold's head was held high by that same leash acting as a noose. In the act of strangling Harry, someone had knocked over the cat kibble, so that's where Rosie was, making the most of a free snack. A scene of quiet chaos. Not one had uttered a peep during the bedlam. Oh, and Harold was bleeding from a two inch gash on his front leg.

With a funky little café tempting me for breakfast, or rather brunch, we stopped for the afternoon. I caught up with the business side of things on the web, sent out emails and photos, and then took the pups for a walk.

The focus in Bandon was on an active fishing scene, ripe for tourists with outdoor patios, flags, signs fluttering in the breeze. I liked it but didn't have that craving to move here but still, not bad, not bad.

Bandon has the usual history of local Native tribes being relocated by force after white settlers, in this case an Irishman, 'discovered' the area and used the US Congress Act to claim land. And yes, gold had been found. Coincidence? Nope.

These days the focus is on tourism, timber, agriculture and the fishing industry with a population of about 3,000 in the last census. The historic downtown was first established in the 1870s but most burned in a huge wild fire during 1936, killing eleven people and causing over $3 million in damages.

Ready for another walk, Harold stood, his legs oddly spaced, and his balance was off. He shook himself, waited a moment, and then walked off normal as ever. Shit. Arthritis? Neurological? Shit. I watched him closely after that and the pattern became his new idea of normal. Pause. Stumble. Pause. Shake. Walk. He's only eight. This worried me.

PACIFIC CITY, OREGON

What can I say? I missed the place. Truly.

We parked on the beach once more and found the scraps of a dying campfire. With odds and ends of timbers found in the dunes, it blazed as we stretched our legs, glad to be back. The clouds hung low but no storm came in.

I'd been obsessed with the State Parks job but heard nothing. It was almost time to head back towards New Mexico. I craved staying but living on this public beach was not a good long-term option, so with maps on lap, the month ahead began to take shape. Disappointed at my lack of sociability, it was clear that the job at Trader Joes had drained me more than expected. My usual travel mode had been of finding local pubs and cafes, getting to know and be known, helping out around the community, none of that had come to be on this trip. What had I been doing instead? Finding new ideas for ways to live, places to make home? I didn't know. A restlessness had been awakened in me, a desire to see how others lived, if only by observing. I'd taken to the back roads with my family of four-legged friends to see where we'd be happiest. Washington Coast was out. The dense rain forest strangled me and the eagles threatened Little Stevie. Montana I'd liked, the open rangeland, the mountains and Flathead Lake. Wyoming, yes, those small towns we'd passed through, the winding blue highways had satisfied a part of me. The bears though? Not so keen. Politics neither.

Oregon. Ah, yes, Oregon. So far so good. The people, the small funky untouched villages found along an empty coast of huge beaches and cragged cliffs. This was my happy place. Time to find a way to move here. I'd found my next home.

CORVALLIS, OREGON

Trader Joes was fairly easy to find after chatting to a few locals in a café out on the western side of town. I'd come in from Newport, a clusterfuck of a tourist town, one to pass through, yet also admirable for its kitsch. Stevie had hidden under the bed; it was all too loud for him. The highway across eastwards was once again Highway 20, the one I'd been on and off since Montana. I'd found some towns online that seemed a good choice with cheap housing, yet close to the ocean but driving through them it was obviously not a good fit; the churches, the political signs, and how the local men stared at us, no not my place. I kept going; it was a long day but okay. With a night in the forest at a little used campground to ground us, we'd hit Corvallis in the early morning. Ideal.

Trader Joes was not. The mates (managers) were negative nellies when I'd told them of possibly transferring.

"Don't do it. Pretentious. Annoying. Horrible. Don't move here. Oh, and it's really expensive."

Seriously? These are the managers, the role models? Wow. It pissed me off. Corvallis had been one of my destination towns to visit, a possible new home as it has TJs, and is close to mountains and within a couple of hours of the coast. Pretty much each of those towns on my list has been a dud. Well, working here, at the store was crossed off my list but the town I liked. We didn't do much but walked around downtown, a place of old buildings, cafes, bars, stores, students, and a ton of locals. What a concept. People walking around town. That doesn't happen in Santa Fe, not really, there's no reason for us locals to go there except in summer for the afternoon music on the plaza. Here in Corvallis, students, tourists, and locals all mixed together, welcomed us, chatted to us as we wandered along the river park, taking photos, and yes shopping while there.

Corvallis is a pretty big town, at least for us on this trip, I'd done well by avoiding the cities, even taking the ferry to bypass Seattle. I was pretty proud of myself for finding the smaller communities, not that they'd all been that friendly, but Corvallis won a star for openness. Well, not the staff at TJs, but everyone else was nice, even the homeless fella in the park who asked to pet the pups and held out his hand for their decision. Rough around the edges, a tad smelly, John had a warm smile and the dogs took to him. We spent a few moments walking along the main road together. A good guy.

SISTERS, OREGON

"Is it always this busy?" I asked at the gas station outside of town, handing the young man a basket of odds and ends.

He looked at me as if I were an idiot. Not a good start. Outside the station had a line of traffic, the parking lot overflowed with trucks, RVs, and travel trailers. The main highway, yes, Hwy 20 again, had brought us through the Willamette National Forest with peaks at Tombstone Summit of 4,236 feet where we'd stopped for a late lunch. Stevie and the pups all took a wander with me down a dirt road into a mountain meadow devastated by wildfires, with thousands of blackened stumps, little grass, and a silence that disconcerted even the cat.

Sisters, Oregon? Huh, I'd not researched this place but leaving the main road and heading into the town, I instantly liked it. Since the Oregon State Parks hadn't offered me a perfect job, I'd started looking around again. Sisters on first impression stood a good chance of welcoming us. Almost too kitsch yet likeable, the town itself is deep within Deschutes National Forest. At an elevation of 3,186, the climate was hot and dry, reminding me of Santa Fe nicely. A high desert landscape of ponderosas, scrubby grasses and little understory, the forest didn't overwhelm me like along the coast. Rainforests freak me out, but this worked.

Damn, I sound desperate, don't I? Let's just say it was time for a change. Although it's a mixed bag. I love my home, built the place myself, just as needed, and it's more of a creative art project more than anything professional. Madrid, New Mexico, is a funky little artist village of a few hundred with many a tourist keeping us alive by buying our books, paintings, sculptures and eating out. Unique. It will be hard to replace, but who's trying to replace it? A change of scene, new conversations, new hikes, the challenge of settling into an unknown lifestyle, that's what was needed and craved. This road trip was to help me whittle down the options. Yeah, right. I'm just desperate.

Anyway, Sisters won a gold star. A funky old historical small town of around 2,000 in the last census, and with so many tourists that finding parking in the afternoons was a nightmare. Mornings in town were quiet and peaceful, the cafes open, a bakery offered the most amazing selection of treats, galleries, and my oh my, a brewery. I was in heaven. The dogs loved it too, as they were welcomed nearly everywhere. We walked the ten block downtown area, stopping for attention, sniffing the posts, and lounging on the grassy parks. Samuel Hindeman homesteaded the city in the 1870s and then opened a post office soon after. Sisters seems to be one of the few towns without the usual history of forcing Native Americans to relocate under threat. It was never an issue here, and there are no stories of major fights, oh and funnily enough there are no mines. Hmm.

We drove up towards Three Creek Lake on a national forest road that began in town, taking us through a neighborhood of trailers and smaller homes tucked in the pines and ponderosas. Heading up into the mountains, we climbed past numerous tracks off to the hills on either side until one caught my eye for no special reason. We pulled off and slowly made our way up another half a mile to find a dispersed camping site hidden in the forest, nicely level and a rock-lined fire pit. Perfect, backing in, checking out the window for bears, I opened the doors. Critters ran free. I lay on the grass and sighed. Yep, just what we needed. No one to bother us and we were still only fifteen minutes from a likable town. No rules, no neighbors, no traffic, this kind of camping is what we all do best. I sighed in relief.

"We're staying here a while. Any complaints?"

"There's no river," Rosie offered, "But that's okay, look, I can run up this hill, hahaha!" And she did, she ran up and over the incline and then popped back to tell me that it was more of the same. "Trees. Lots of them."

"I love trees!" Stevie shouted from twenty feet up in the air, "I love trees! Can we live here?"

Harold dug a hole under a tree trunk, head buried deep in the soft dirt, he obviously liked it. I set up the fire for later, kindling and dead wood lay all around. With the table unfolded, and dinner warming on the stove, then I dozed.

Three Creeks Lake: I had no idea what a delight this little lake would be, on a Sunday too, full of families, paddle boats, and kayaks. Only ten miles up NF 16 to the Tam McArthur Rim, we came across cars, trucks, and cyclists parked alongside the pond with snow-capped mountains in the background, and the water reflected the clear sky above, a glassy azure. The sun shone. Families camped out. Kids played. Dogs paddled. And there was even a tiny house selling ice cream, books and beer. I was in heaven, Stevie not so much. Kitty Lockdown #45.

Three Creeks Lake had only 28 acres of water, but offered two small campgrounds, which were both mostly full yet a few places came open as we hiked the trail counter-clockwise. Briefly tempted, I'd remember Stevie and forget about it, the dispersed campsite in the trees was better for all of us, better for Stevie that's for sure. Broken Top Mountain rose to 9,175 feet, a craggy face watching over this summer frivolity. The trail suddenly stopped though, a sharp rise in the land into old growth forests made it impossible to hike around the pond completely so we back-tracked, and holding my sandals I splashed in the tepid water, loving this afternoon in the wilderness. Yep, I did like Sisters. I could live here. Haven't I said that already?

Three Sisters Brewery helped. Although not really my style of pub, it was too large, modern, and focused on tourist family dining, the smaller side bar appealed with more of a local informal pub feel. I sat at the counter and ordered a beer and pizza. My treat. Chatting to Eden on my right, I wish I hadn't started, as he was a bore, a negative tourist-hating man in his sixties. Sheesh. I was only being friendly. With the pizza in front of me, conversation ended, thankfully. The TV gained his attention, not me wiping cheese of my chin.

Presents. I needed presents and being a cheap bugger, I bought ten koozies to hand out, two for me obviously, but a few to hand out. Did you get one? Sorry. I only had twenty bucks cash on me.

BEND, OREGON

Much bigger and busier than expected, I never did find the places seen in photos online. It wasn't bad, mind, just much busier than hoped for. We drove downtown through road works, stopping at TJs where an easy-going lass chatted to me happily, another transplant. She loved it, her and the family had moved there from Portland, Maine, and wouldn't think of moving back. The heat, mountains, rivers, all of it was 'perfect' as far as she was concerned. Oh, and she finished by introducing me to a manager called Tim, saying happily that I might be moving there.

"Really, that's great! We're always open to transfers, especially from one of the busiest stores in the States. You'd be welcome here, Sarah. Let me know if you're coming and I'll talk to the Captain for you." Tim shook my hand warmly.

Sherry gave me directions downtown to the river and historic area.

That was that. I left soon after; we'd walked around the park on the river, stumbled around the three or four blocks of businesses and then hit the road. I preferred Sisters, but we could live there and commute into Bend, right? Food for thought.

BOISE, IDAHO

"Where are we, Hawold?"

Stevie sat on his back legs and looked out the window. Rosie sat next to him, both staring at the freeway and the kids playing in the swimming pool. The air conditioning hummed and rumbled. I lay on another bed with Harold. He explained motels to them both.

"It's a strange smelling yet curiously relaxing place for Sarah. I remember the first time I stayed in a motel, oh, long before you were born, either of you."

They glanced at him and then stared back out the window.

"Yes, it was a little much for me, I admit. The floors were some odd slippery substance and my feet slid and splayed. I simply couldn't walk. Sarah had to pick me up and carry me into the room. Much like she did with you, Stevie. Although, I wasn't in a crate."

"It's so busy out there. Are we staying, Hawold? I could watch this all day long. I can't smell them though." Stevie looked at me, sprawled on the bed, half asleep with stress and heat. It had been a long day. "Oh, I guess we are."

We had driven through from Bend in temperatures in the high nineties, too hot to stop and camp anywhere, the hills were on fire, mountain passes closed down, and even stopping for gas was an issue. I'd stopped finally on the interstate, gone inside for the bathroom and to get ice and soda. By the time I was back in the van, ten minutes at most, the pets were panting hard, lethargic and lying on the floor. The van was even parked in the shade of the building. Panicked to see them suffer so, I'd hit the highway and aimed for Wyoming again. The Grand Tetons sounded just right with temps in the seventies and low eighties. I drove hundreds of miles, stopping in Boise for the night, too exhausted to carry on. I'd remembered a motel by the airport, fairly cheap and dog friendly.

"I have two dogs and a cat. Is that okay?"

A young but rather large and doughy man sat behind the counter sporting tattoos and a pierced nose; he shrugged. "There's a two pet policy. Sorry."

"I can't leave them in the van, they'd die of heat exhaustion. Please? I'll keep the cat in his crate. Please? I can't drive any further today, I really can't."

He looked at me, worn out and red-eyed, desperate admittedly. "Okay, keep the cat crated and don't leave the dogs alone in there, okay Miss? That's going to be $79.50. Visa or MasterCard?"

I didn't blink. I didn't care.

With arms full with pet food, a litter box, Stevie in a crate, and two dogs on a leash, I wandered down the hallways, hoping Harold wouldn't need to be carried like last time. They'd carpeted the place thankfully, dirty and stained, but with all the four-paw traction he needed. I had no complaints. In our ground floor room, with the door locked, the critters were free to sniff, drink cool water, and eat dinner. With the TV on, after a shower for me, I collapsed, out cold for an hour or more despite the traffic flying past near by. The youngsters were fascinated with the view. Harold liked the cold moist floor in the bathroom. It was a good time for all.

And then I swam. With the pets left out free in the room, and Stevie locked in the bathroom, terrified he'd get out somehow and panic with all the traffic, I swam.

Outside in ninety-eight degree weather, I swam back
and forth, then circling the pool, breaststroke,
backstroke, and just paddling. Submerged in cool water
revived me, just what was needed. Worth $79.50.

At Trader Joes the next day, it was time to stock up for
a week back in Wyoming as Boise was just too hot for
us, especially Little Stevie, who once back in the van
began panting despite the air conditioning. A cart full of
pet food, snacks, beer and a couple of meals, I did the
usual introduction at the cashier's desk, partly to get my
crew discount, but also to test the waters. Friendly
manager, easy chatting with the cashier who'd moved
there from Texas. Definitely welcoming. Although the
climate put me off, our morning in the old historic
downtown was interesting enough, walking around
three story red brick buildings, finding a café with great
breakfasts and quick Internet with shaded parking for
Van Dreamy and residents. I'd been here some years
before on a small book tour and had done exactly the
same thing. Motel. Downtown. Walk Harold. Eat.
Leave. It was nothing personal.

JACKSON, WYOMING

Back tracking didn't seem so bad. I'd told myself to find a loop, a circular route on this trip but no; the idea of camping in Utah in August was beyond me. Looking up temperatures on the web, Jackson Hole was just right. Plus I might bump into Frank. We took two days getting there, one on the Interstate, stopping to gas up only once and even that was too much for the critters, all panting and struggling in the heat. I'd kept going, drinking cold sodas from the iced cooler, windows up, air conditioning blasting, we made it into Wyoming finally. Straight through town and up into the National Forest, there was a perfect spot waiting for us.

Elk Reserve, one of a few national preserves and based in Jackson Hole, is home to more than 6,000 elk over the winter months before heading to high ground for summer. I didn't see a single one and now I know why. East of the highway and onto North Elk Refuge Road, it was easy enough to find from the historic district, and a graded road took us climbing up higher and higher up the east side of the valley up into the Gros Ventre Range. Seeing a couple of tents tucked away on the ridge facing the Tetons, we pulled off under a lodge pole pine on a level spot with trampled grass and a cold fire pit. Yep.

The view was incredible: Across the flat valley north of Jackson we looked down from one mountain peak over to the Tetons on a clear bright but cool evening. Stevie pounced on flies in the tall grass. The pups explored and chased each other across a meadow. Time for dinner, a much needed cold beer, and yes, I could live here. It's kind of an epiphany after living in one place over twenty years, calling New Mexico home despite the constant travels off and on. Jackson did appeal in many ways, with a small funky downtown, tourism for income, mountains and hiking, skiing, biking for time off, and yes, a microbrewery or two. Not bad. Not bad at all. The pets liked it too. That helps.

Work, it was time to think about finding meaning in my work. Doing the same old in and out drove me insane. Well, it depressed me really. The routine, and a lack of stimulus drained me, that and the inane questions and jokes from the customers at Trader Joes.

"Where are you from? What a pretty accent you have. Is this apple gluten free? Welcome to America! Welcome to New Mexico! Where is the cheese?"

Yeah, right, I'm a foreigner. Somehow it doesn't piss me off as much when on the road, it's to be expected almost, but in a town I've lived near for over twenty years? Can't stand it. And now, someone will make that 'pretty accent' joke after reading this, and I'll smile sweetly and move along. Just saying…you'll owe me a drink.

Meaning in work: We all have different needs and focus in general and at work too, right? Well, I'm bored by my job, that's obvious. It's a dead-end job unless you want to climb the short and competitive ladder. Me, I'm not interested in working 50 hours a week in a grocery store, not that there's anything wrong with it. I mean that. It's one of the most needed jobs, that and trash removal, we'd be lost without either these days considering how few of us grow our own food or know how to recycle and reuse to the point of creating as little trash as possible. For me, Trader Joes is not enough of a challenge, it's not engaging either brains or creativity. Landscaping had been good for that, designing, billing, and keeping customers and crew happy. Yep, but the knees gave out, saying a loud and definitive 'no'. Fair enough. It's a sense of accomplishment, the act of production from scratch that I like, whether building my home or writing a book or an article. Create and be done with it! Income alone is not enough anymore, so it's time to question values, attitudes, and preferences for the years ahead. Is this a midlife crisis but without the kids leaving to make an empty nest?

"Right, Harold? You're not leaving me, are you?"

Harold sat up, and stuck his tongue out. Stevie pounced on me from behind a clump of grass. "I'm not going anywhere! I love this! What a great life, I love this, I love you…"

"Ouch! That hurts…" as he latched onto my wrist with claws and teeth. He looked up surprised, hanging upside down with a trickle of blood on his mouth. "Oh sorry. I get excited."

I'd be happy in a job that takes me out and about, to a new place each day if possible. Less drained by constant superficial conversations would be ideal, not that I don't like talking to folks, kind of like it really, but not about the ingredients of that can of soup. Tell me about where you're from, why you left, what inspires you. Flexible enough to chat, to wander off, and finish projects on my own timeline. Sounds like it's time to quit Trader Joes, doesn't it? Scary, the income is the best thing about having a proper job. It's addictive. Easy. But draining. Something has to change.

Why not consider writing as work? Career? I've been doing it long enough, what with publishing books and articles, and even winning a couple of awards, so why dismiss myself as a writer? I shook my head and went to bed, unsettled by such an obvious question. The days passed quietly up on that hill. We didn't go anywhere, just lay around, stretched, walked, and ate often. The critters loved it. My brain hurt. Too much thinking and not enough answers. Time to move on. Distraction? Or deadlines?

CLARK, COLORADO

Doing up to ten sun salutations each morning has helped my lower back and hips, tight after driving straight through from Jackson. A long days' drive was no longer too hard on the family; they all knew to doze until the engine stopped and doors opened. Back to Elk River north of Steamboat Springs was where we ended up. What a difference a few months makes, as the river flowed gently past, shallow and welcoming on a hot afternoon, it was no longer a raging torrent of timbers and ice. Stripping off, it was a challenge to lie down in the snowmelt even so, but with a shriek and blaming my mum for getting us to do just that in the Pyrenees as kids, I did it. Fully submerged for ten seconds. The best I could do. Rosie paddled, trying to catch little bitty twigs flowing past. Harold drank at the bank with Stevie on a rock copying his big brother. Idyllic.

How will it be to return to life, as I knew it, in New Mexico? A tenant had moved out of the old school bus and studio. Trader Joes expected me back. The local tavern will be unchanged nor the conversations. "Oh, you got new socks? Did I tell you about…"

I lingered in the grassy shade of Colorado and read my travel notes, curious to see what themes came up in my wanderings and wonderings. Work. Home. Relocation. Goals. Little about the act of writing. Why not? It's something I have always done, perhaps that's why? It's such a part of me, like brushing my teeth, walking the pups, why would I question it? The writing comes easily, and it's a way to make sense of the world. Noting down conversations, weather, campsites, and routes, makes it all stick in memory. For me that is. Sorry, if I'm meant to struggle but words flow out easily: It's what to do with them afterwards that is a struggle. After five books though, I'm getting the hang of it, but why not think of dedicating myself to a career as a writer? Stop dabbling? Stop spending 30 hours a week inside a grocery store or a state park?

The fire flickered and died out slowly. The critters were fast asleep inside Van Dreamy but my mind wouldn't shut up, couldn't stop beating me up for such an oversight. Yes, write, focus, write, send out, edit, ask for help, and publish. Publish. Publish.

WILLIAMS CREEK, COLORADO

A rough day followed by a rough night: On Wolf Creek Pass, Rosie puked twice, quietly on her seat behind me, and then stood there nervously as we rolled over the winding San Juan Mountain ranges. A sharp noxious smell alerted me to this, not Rosie herself, she was unusually silent. Harold kept his eyes averted, staring at the birds in the conifers lining the highway. Stevie slept most of the day until it was time to clean up and wipe down the leather seats and rinse off a carpet. Then he decided it was a good time for a walk next to this busy highway. Grabbed and deposited back inside his crate, Stevie sulked. Rosie's day didn't get much better; she wanted to curl up on my lap as we drove. Not a good idea at the best of times, but in these mountains? Hell no.

"Please? My tummy hurts." She worked it for another ten minutes before making Harold share the bed. Poor sods. It's been a long few days. Months. That night, every groan or moan by one of the pets had me reaching for a flashlight, "are you okay?"

"No, I'm not! I want to go outside! I'm tired of this van; I really want to get outside. Please?" Stevie begged all night long, scratching at window screens and then sitting on my head.

At Teal campsite by William's Creek Reservoir, we were lucky enough to claim one of the last sites overlooking clear water and craggy mountains. The lake is stocked with trout but since fishing isn't my thing, who cared? To the east is Indian Head peak, so named for the profile against an azure skyline of alpine mountains. Clouds hovered and dimmed the evening light, sending us all to bed earlier than normal. Only Stevie complained.

The sunrise that next morning over the lake was incredible; melon, peach, orange, pear, apples and grapes, all the colors of a fruit market in the whispers of fine clouds around the grey blue mountains. Just us. The other campers were still hidden in their RVs. I bundled up and made coffee outside over a campfire. Little Stevie was in heaven with trees, grass, and water, and nothing else to scare the bugger, so he wandered around, meowed when he lost sight of me, and ran back under the van when I called, *anyone hungry*?

North of Pagosa Springs is this wonderful haven, it's far along a well-graded national forest road that takes you in to the San Juan Mountains, past dispersed camping areas, hiking trails, fishing spots along the river, and three NF campgrounds. Teal is by far my favorite campground, being small with only 20 or so sites, and overlooking such deep blue water and tall steep sided mountains that my camera is full of images in the changing light and dark. The hills are full of aspens, cottonwoods and ponderosa, with huge open valleys and incredible views from the many hiking trails. Elk, brown bears, eagles, hawks, and deer live in these hills. I've been going there for years, little by little finding new rivers, creeks, and waterfalls. I can't get enough of the place. Summer, especially in July and August, is one of the busiest camping seasons yet still we hiked around the lake and didn't bump into anyone. A lone kayaker drifted past with fishing rod in hand, he nodded at us but said nothing. His camouflage outfit didn't quite work on a pond, but oh well, he was dry and warm, I guess. I hiked in the morning cool weather, listening out for bears. Yep, bear country. A whistle in hand and bells on the dogs' collars, footsteps loud, and singing as much as a non-musical person can, we scrambled around three quarters of the lake before hitting a swamp and turning back.

Soaking in the hot springs in Pagosa, a young man in his early twenties joined me, smiling and happy to be there on that sunny Saturday. We started chatting. Mark was taller than me at six foot, skinny and tanned in his cut-off denim shorts, an outdoor hiker mountain biker type. He told me of his brown van, but he didn't tell me what kind, and I thought it was women who only notice color not engine size? Anyway, Mark had bought the brown van in New Jersey a couple of months ago and had been slowly wandering westward. A happy fella, but he then started to avoid my eyes, slow down the questions, that is until a couple in their sixties joined us. They're in a Sprinter (white) that's fully decked out with wood paneling and working kitchen units. Mark relaxed and chatted up a storm. Am I that strange middle-aged woman now? Yes, the answer is yes. Sadly, yes.

Pagosa Springs Brewery has changed, not for the better. What was a small local's focused brewpub with picnic tables under towering ponderosas is now a warehouse with multiple TV screens and a circus tent with long wooden tables down the center for 'outside seating'. I hated it. The beer was good, and the fish tacos amazing, yet the place has lost a customer. There's just no character unless you call fake lodge/ warehouse a style?

Van Dreamy was still pretty simple inside even after living in it for three months. To think of all that could be done, given my carpentry skills, plumbing, and electric etc., but the simplicity worked still, and was peaceful somehow. Yet I fiddled with it while in Pagosa, checking out the thrift stores, looking for that perfect desk, as the only challenge had been to write inside the van. In the meantime though, I took the extra chair out. Stevie's folded cat crate (three foot by three foot) was set up permanently with the side door rolled up for access, and placed into the space made by removing the extra chair. Rosie disapproved. Within that larger crate I put another small cat carrier, a covered litter box, and a cooler to the side of them both.

I wandered in and out of thrift stores looking for a small cabinet or desk to modify but not seen the one wanted so it was back to the van with a new metal tabletop, to be laid across Stevie's soft crate and it became a place to set up the Coleman stove for making coffee inside on a rainy day. Perfect now we're in the high desert of the Southwest, right? Funnily enough it worked: Colorado that week had been sunny all day long until four or five when the rains came down hard. We hunkered down inside and enjoyed the pinging against the roof. Anyway, the kitchen drawers were to the right and the cooler could be used as a bench while cooking. Rosie liked to cuddle next to me, so she and I lay in the back on the bed during the rains, Stevie on his shelf above my head, and Harold claimed the driver's seat.

Writing in the afternoons became easier with the new set up. Time to ponder the last few months in the Northwest, to review my time on the road. How can I just up and go like this though? Didn't you want to ask? And why would I? Well, let's blame my parents for taking us everywhere in the old Rover and Volvos. I also blame my friend Shaun for reminding me of the restlessness inside me. And I thank Casey for sitting me down at the computer one day as we played online, her showing me how to make an income from writing, editing, and just talking about what we both do and love. But at the time I didn't take her seriously. After this trip, the wandering mind and winding roads have wakened me, seeing new ways of living. What will life and routine do to this mind shift? What will Trader Joes be like? Can I even go back to work there? Daunted by the possibilities, I made coffee and sat by the fire in the damp evenings, watching Stevie hunt squirrels with the pups.

Once settled back in Van Dreamy that last night at Teal campground, I sat at the new table with my laptop, and wrote up notes for an editing job, then checked my photographs, deleting many, and read a few nonfiction essays by Joan Didion.

It was time for another mug of tea with a last walk down to the river, another log on the fire, and a broad grin under a hidden moon: *I'm a writer*. This is my life now. Camping, driving, writing, I can do it after all. Why did it take me so long though? Fear. Laziness. A resigned focus on home and job. It wore me down. This though, with quiet times in the van, reading, writing, and sending out proposals and ideas, this life wakes me up. But what will next week bring? Next month? Where will we be? A slight frost yesterday morning in the mountains was quite a reminder that winter is coming fast. September, October, camping in October is doable in the van but still it's daunting, at least at this elevation. Back to my cabin in New Mexico then was next on the list, the sensible list not the dreamer's one. But if someone rents my place for winter, we could head south perhaps? The Gila National Forest? Arizona? Louisiana? Or Alabama? I've not been to Alabama yet and that's as good a reason as any in my book. Why not, eh?

Packing up for the final leg heading home in the early morning cool, the camp host wandered over with notebook in hand.

"Is that your cat?"

He tucked in a tight green shirt to his pressed blue jeans and pulled out a pen from his back pocket. His was a weasely face and squinting eyes that held no humor. The broad-rimmed felt hat didn't help.

Stevie, the little darling, ran past us and jumped inside the van, and then hid under the bed. "Yup."

"Well, I need to write you up. Pets need to be leashed. He's been hunting birds. It's not acceptable." He paused.

Our last day on the road and Stevie finally gets us in trouble? Funny. Oh, and it was squirrels he stalked. "Oh really? A ticket? For a cat?"

Harold and Rosie wandered over to see what the fuss was about, both unleashed. The host pulled out his notepad with a flourish and licked the tip of the pen leaving a bruised stain drip on his pursed lips and nodded solemnly.

"Right." I picked up my cowboy hat, nodded at the camp host, and then wandered down to the water's edge. The dogs sprang around me, startling ducks into loud squawking with Harold in chase mode. Rosie's bum stuck out of a hole, ignoring us all as she dug a tunnel back to Oregon.

"I hate you! I hate you! Don't leave me!" Stevie sprang out of the van and raced through the grass towards me. "What are you doing? Don't leave me! Don't leave me!"

EPILOGUE

"How much did you spend on gas? How many miles did you drive? What did the campgrounds cost? Did you need mechanical work? How much did the van cost?"

We're a practical bunch. We want facts and figures. None of this anecdotal crap. Just the facts. Well, some of my friends are scientists, statisticians, more focused on the details than the stories. Me, I'm more of an impressionist than realist, but this is for the rest of you. And no, I didn't total and summarize any of it. That's your job. I was too busy dipping fingers and toes in mountain lakes, paddling on ocean beaches, and worrying about a cat called Stephen.

The numbers of
- $ spent on mechanics: 716
- times (each day) I thought I'd lost the cat: 8
- scars on my left hand from grabbing cat and throwing him back in the van: 5
- times Harold had diarrhea in the van: 2
- miles driven on Interstates: 346
- times I spilt coffee in the van: 2
- weeks on the road: 11
- motel cost: 79.50

- campground fees: 236
- times I stepped in diarrhea in the van: 2
- cold plunges in alpine lakes: 6
- nights spent in a motel: 1
- books read: 47
- $ spent on laundry: 54
- walks per day with dogs and cat: 3
- walks per day with just the dogs: 3
- times I bought gas: 26
- miles driven: 7843
- times I was scared: 1
- $ spent on firewood: 15
- $ in the weekly envelope (budget): 150
- times I overspent my budget: 6
- weeks spent on the Oregon Coast: 3
- nights slept on the beach: 5
- times Rosie puked in the van: 2
- Gallons of gas used: 409

and lastly, the number of $ spent on the road trip: just
enough to have a blast.

I'd do it again. Wouldn't you?

ABOUT THE AUTHOR

Sarah Leamy was the boring little sister who suddenly left her English life and became the broke nomadic wanderer and writer. As a socially awkward and insecure Brit abroad, she lived first in Europe and then crossed the States and into Guatemala, performing, writing and working odd jobs as she explored new countries alone or with Daisy, her slightly grumpy Border Collie. Since then her essays, articles, and novels have been published in the UK and USA. She was a finalist in 2014 and her novels won twice in the New Mexico/ Arizona Book Awards in 2012 and 2016.

She now travels and writes from a 2003 Dodge Conversion Van with Harold, Rosie, and Stevie. It's a good life. And yes, she did quit her job.

www.sarahleamy.com

www.dirtroadsanddogs.com

www.instagram.com/dirtroadsanddogs

Made in the USA
Middletown, DE
15 April 2022

64275015R00116